D0385176

# The Little Book
## of

# FENG

# SHUI

*Dedicated to*
*Alan Hunter*

The Little Book
of

# FENG

# SHUI

*by*

*J.M. SERTORI*

SIENA

This edition published and distributed
by Siena, 1998, reprinted 1999

Siena is an imprint of Parragon

Parragon
Queen Street House
4 Queen Street
Bath BA1 1HE

Produced by Magpie Books, an imprint of
Robinson Publishing Ltd, London

ISBN 0 75252 690 1

A copy of the British Library Cataloguing-in-
Publication Data is available from the British Library
Printed in China

# Contents

❀

## PART TWO

## FENG SHUI IN PRACTICE

# Introduction

It is one of the most well-known sectors of Chinese thought, but nobody really knows what it is. Media pundits talk about its properties, but can't even agree how to pronounce it. Will it make your life better? Will it make your life endurable? Or will it make your life a misery as you endlessly fret about the positioning of your furniture and the color of your walls?

This is feng shui, the ancient, immutable laws of the universe that are constantly revised, bent and broken every day. You can't do this, you must do that. Do such-and-such a thing and you will have good fortune. Do such-and-such a thing and you will be doomed, unless you also do ten other things.

Part of the confusion surrounding feng

shui comes from its manifold origins. There is no canonical book or almanac that can answer all your questions on feng shui, and there is no single school that trains the world's feng shui masters.

Feng shui has grown over many centuries, by trial and error, observation and superstition. At one level, there is little more to feng shui than a random collection of old wives' tales, at another, it is one of the oldest sciences known to mankind. Like all collections of philosophy, some of it clearly works. Other parts require a leap of faith. If you find that you understand some parts, but others seem insane, then you are in good company.

### The First Science

In recent years, the people of the West have taken an interest in ecology and conservation. They have stopped trying to force the natural world to conform to the will of mankind, and started trying to live in harmony with it. But this has been part of feng shui for thousands of years. Modern times have brought an attempt to set feng shui principles down in stone, but there is no Great Answer to tie up all the loose ends. Some practitioners set special store in the points of the compass. Others prefer to emphasise colors and decoration. Still more use astrology and divination. This book cannot cover all the angles, but it can introduce the basics.

The words "feng shui" mean "wind and water," those things which can be felt but not seen, grasped but not held. Or at least, that is what a large number of Chinese people say. But an equally large number disagree. They claim "feng shui" refers not to the unfathomable qualities of natural phenomena, but to wind and water as forces of achievement. The wind rushes up a mountain and through the grasses. The waves crash in upon the shore. They are both symbols of the elements, and of humanity's constant desire to better itself. Feng shui is all these things. Feng shui is none of them.

## Form and Compass

*Like the constant interplay of yin and yang, the dark and light that balances all things, feng shui eventually settled down into two schools, the Form school of object and abstract fortunes, and the Compass school, which relied upon lucky and unlucky directions. They are quite different, and it is the unceremonial shoving together of these ideas that has confused many readers. The most complex, mathematical theories of Compass feng shui are beyond the scope of this Little Book, since they would require a substantially larger number of pages, and a computer to store the thousands of different almanac entries and exceptions to the rules. This book is primarily about the Form school, although it too mixes many different elements.*

*Anyone with an interest in feng shui must ask themselves how seriously they are going to take it. Because there are so many competing authorities, much feng shui lore seems contradictory and some of it makes no sense at all.*

This book will take you through the formation of feng shui in the distant past, and show you how it developed. It will also show you the way feng shui looks today, as a farmer's guide to good crop rotation gradually turned into a manual for town planning, a horror story about the spirit world and a guide for interior decoration. Feng shui is all these things and more. What it means to you, is ultimately your decision.

Feng shui began when people had a very different way of explaining the world. A seismologist will tell you not to build your house in an earthquake zone, because you will be close to a geological fault line where the tectonic plate is apt to shift again. A feng shui master will tell you that there is a restless dragon beneath the surface. Both the seismologist and the feng shui master agree that building in an earthquake zone is a bad idea, they just have different ways of explaining it. In their own way, they are both right.

There are a lot of feng shui rules that even

real skeptics have trouble disputing. It is perfectly reasonable to argue that a house in a quiet neighborhood will have happier occupants than one in a noisy, smoky street. Feng shui masters will argue that a motorway flyover near your house will throw bad qi at you, but is that really such a far cry from a scientist showing you that carbon monoxide levels from car exhausts will increase the chances of illness if you live close to a busy road?

As you read this book, you may find many places where you feel yourself drawing a line between sense and superstition. One idea may be perfectly reasonable, but another might be nothing more than a silly pun, and one which loses all resonance and meaning in translation. It might be an interesting fact to know about the Chinese language, but is it likely to affect your fate?

The threshold of the twenty-first century is the best and worst of times for feng shui. It has finally achieved world-wide recognition, and an incredible level of popularity, as demonstrated by the vast numbers of books published on the subject. Despite the paltry number of Chinese novels available in English and the tiny handful of films, you can go into any bookshop and trip over a dozen feng shui books. It has become as ubiquitous as Chinese food, but it has also become as diluted.

There is no such thing in Chinese as "chop suey," the very word is an Americanism. The many quick-and-ready Chinese concoctions available in supermarkets are nothing like the Chinese food they eat in China. They are foreign imitations, partially understood and badly thrown together. This, unfortunately, is also the way that feng shui may find itself going. The problem with being the trend of the moment is that the moment can fade all too quickly and become yesterday's news.

Feng shui is Chinese, but you only have to hear people arguing how to pronounce it to realise that there is more to it than that. In Mandarin Chinese, it is pronounced "fung shway". In south China, around the Hong Kong area where they speak the Cantonese dialect, it is pronounced "fong shoy". Either of these versions is acceptable, but not an amalgam of both. The current English habit of pronouncing it "feng shooey" (to rhyme with "chop suey") is simply incorrect. If a "feng shooey expert" does not know enough about their subject to say it properly, by all means listen to what they have to say, but be careful if they ask you for money for a consultation.

Feng shui has existed for thousands of years, but even in China its position is under threat. This is because its many achievements have been co-opted by newer, more acceptable disciplines, imported from the dynamic West: sociology, psychology, architecture, geography, ergonomics; feng shui reached many similar conclusions centuries before. As each new discipline claims to know everything about a little part of our lives, feng shui's share of the original knowledge gets smaller and smaller. Perhaps one day, it will have only the weird superstitions left. This book is also here to remind you that, while some feng shui may look a little strange today, in its time it was the best explanation avaiable.

Modern thought often reaches the same conclusions as feng shui. Social geography tells us that farming communities like to face south because their crops get more sunlight. Large companies have spent vast amounts of money on time-and-motion studies to increase their workers' productivity, only to reach the same conclusions as thousand-year-old feng shui manuals. Sitting too close to the office exit can be a distraction for a busy worker because of the noise outside and the constant comings and goings of others. A feng shui master would have said much the same thing, but couched in more magical terms.

Meteorologists and psychologists tell us that people's moods are affected by the weather, and talk of illnesses like Seasonal Affective Disorder where people can get depressed at the onset of winter. And the cures that they prescribe? Natural light in your house, balanced decor (neither too bright nor too dark), and an even temperature throughout. You would find exactly the same suggestions in a feng shui manual, but you could have found them a thousand years before Seasonal Affective Disorder was a twinkle in the doctor's eye.

This book examines the simplest areas of feng shui, the very basic principles of luck design and warding-off of evil. It will tell you something about the situation of your house in its environment, and many of the key points that may influence your fortune. For convenience of use, it is divided into two sections, one for reading and one for reference. The first section will explain how feng shui came to be, and the second will give you a few tips on how to put it to work immediately in your own life.

With this book, you can ensure that your house is in a harmonious environment, and answer some of the simpler questions about its layout and decoration. You will be able to use the points of the compass to determine which parts of your home influence different areas of your luck and life, and take basic steps to improve them with charms and colors. You may also notice that several everyday aspects of your domestic or professional life have been subjected to adverse influences you were not previously aware of.

If you are inspired to look further into this mysterious world, there are plenty of other books on the subject that cover more specialized areas and explain certain ideas and laws in much greater detail. There is also a growing number of courses and feng shui practitioners who will teach you how to get actively involved, and will professionally advise you on the feng shui of your home or workplace. Feng shui may be the trend of the moment, but there has never before been as much information available in the English language as there is now. If you've never heard of feng shui, you've picked the best time to start learning about it.

PART ONE

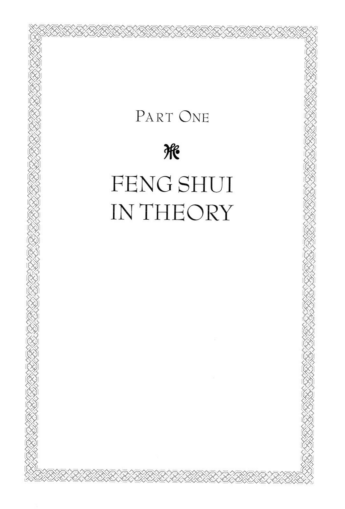

# FENG SHUI
# IN THEORY

# HOW TO BE CHINESE

China hasn't had an Emperor for years. But China and Chinese thought grew out of a world that did. And according to that worldview, China is the center of everything. Even its proper name "Zhongguo" means "The Middle Kingdom". The Chinese Emperor is the ruler of everything under heaven, in other words, he is the ruler of the world.

This may come as something of a surprise to you, but as far as the Chinese feng shui masters are concerned, the rulers of your country are merely underlings of the Emperor. They must pay him regular tribute, and do what they are told. China is the center, and all other nations are mere reflections of China's glory. China may not be ruled by the Son of Heaven any more, but it still calls itself the Middle

Kingdom. How big is the Middle Kingdom? It is everything under heaven ("Tian xia"), or in other words, the whole planet. We are all Chinese. It's just that many of the barbarian nations of the West have not realized it yet.

Even to Westerners, China is not just the area on the map in the East of Asia. It also includes many "foreign" countries. Manchuria, Mongolia, Taiwan, Tibet are all, or have once been, parts of China. Chinese people take China with them wherever they go. They are Chinese people first, united by their language and belief. Their citizenship of America, Britain, Canada, Malaysia, and so on comes a very distant second place. A third of the world's population speaks Chinese, and feng shui is part of their heritage.

According to Chinese popular superstition, the Supreme Being is not to be bothered by mere mortals. Only the Emperor is qualified to pray to the most powerful gods, we underlings must settle for spirits and ghosts at our own social level. And like us, these creatures don't have much power. They can pull a few strings, call in a few favors or roll up their sleeves and get to work, but they could do with a little spiritual support. Feng shui is designed to make your guardian angels feel at home in your home. It makes their lives just that little bit easier, and the benefit will rub off on you.

But how did the Chinese grow to believe in these spirits and their powers? What led them to look at the world in this way, and what relevance does it have today? When modern, city-dwelling people in our country decide to paint their front doors a new color because of this "great new thing" called feng shui, they are only the most recent successors of an ancient tradition. Before them were Chinese immigrants, before them Chinese city-dwellers, before them were generation upon generation of rural Chinese, all the way back to a time before records were properly kept. And since we've now reached the beginning, let us start ...

# LIFE ON THE FARM

The modern Chinese are the inheritors of the mystical lore of feng shui, but they are not all that different from us. Many of the superstitions and ideas of feng shui are common in many other cultures, but in order to find them we must look back in time to the days when our ancestors and the Chinese were virtually identical.

Many centuries ago, the common people of China lived on the land. They tended their flocks and looked after their crops, which is always a never-ending task. One of the reasons that China is such a large political entity, even in ancient times, is that the risk of flood and famine, and the vast distances between certain important resources made it necessary to establish rule over far-flung areas. Crops can be grown in one place, but the flood plains of the rivers were, and are, volatile. Coal has to come from another area, but one which cannot support crops. If the inhabitants wanted both food and fuel, they had to cooperate, and integrate.

Food, of course, was of major concern, as it was in all early cultures. In the modern, developed world, we often take it for granted, not only that distant farmers are working on the land to stock our supermarkets, but that the supermarkets are policing the produce to ensure it doesn't turn bad and kill us. Country living might seem simple from the outside, but it can be very complicated. Anyone can throw a few seeds on the ground and hope that they grow. But how do you grow enough food so that you have enough to eat? These days, it is mostly somebody else's problem, but in ancient times, it was an everyday line between life and death.

Most of us buy food with money, but we earn money by doing jobs that were not necessary in the ancient world. This has meant that many of us have been alienated from the fundamental concerns that created feng shui, because the modern world provides for us so easily. But back then, if you did not own a cow and you needed milk, you needed to get some from your neighbors. In that case, you had to grow surplus food so that you had something to barter with your neighbors in exchange. Early feng shui was built around such concerns, because without them, there would have been no progress at all.

But the early Chinese people had time on their side. They began to notice a few things happening over and over again. These days we take a lot of them for granted because we think they are obvious, but someone had to be the first to notice. The sun rises in the morning and sets in the evening. Days get longer and longer until the middle of summer, then shorter and shorter until the middle of winter. Winter is cold, summer is hot. It seems so obvious now, but there was a time in the distant past when somebody was the first to notice. That person was one of the first feng shui masters.

# Planting Time

In China, as in most other cultures, the leap to civilisation required agriculture. The day that a group of people start farming and animal husbandry instead of aimlessly wandering in search of prey, they become much more powerful. With a single home, they become more territorial. With arable land, they become more productive. With more production, they become more populous. And with a larger population, they have more spare individuals to help out on the farm, specialize in new industries or simply sit and watch the world go by. Watching the world go by was an important component in early feng shui.

When do you plant your crops? Spring, of course. Just look at the way that things grow in the natural world. Buds blossom in spring, fruit grows through the summer, and then it falls when it's ripe and ready. If you want to be a successful farmer, you must imitate nature from the first day on. That way, you wouldn't have to worry about the terrible cold of winter, and when your crops needed the most sunlight, it would be summer and the days would be long and warm. Your crops would be ready to harvest at the beginning of autumn, round about the time that we now call September.

The more a farming community is in tune with nature, the better prepared it is to deal with hardships. It is the world's agricultural communities that invented primitive weather forecasting, that looked for patterns in the stars and watched the moon as it waxed and waned. As the wisdom of the farmers benefited the population as a whole, the feng shui masters were asked to explain other things about the way the world worked. It is these explanations that have gradually

coalesced into the philosophy we call
feng shui.

# EARLY FENG SHUI
# AT WORK

❀

So how do the concerns of ancient farmers relate to us today, and what part do they play in feng shui? To answer that question, we have to take a hypothetical problem, and guess how it might have been answered by the precursors of today's feng shui masters. As you might expect, it is about planting crops.

Let us imagine that the farmers have started planting their crops at the right time. But some are getting better crops than others. If they were to ask a feng shui master for the answer, what would he have to say? Farmer A lives close to the lake, so when he waters his crops, he doesn't have to walk quite so far. He doesn't get so tired, he gets more work done, and so his crops are in a better condition. But how about Farmer B? He lives close to the lake too, but his crops are not doing very well. It can't be a problem with water, so what is it?

Could it be evil spirits? No, he can't see any. How about the soil in the fields? He picks up a handful from each field and looks at them. Nope, they look exactly the same. So what is it? Birds stealing the food? No, the feng shui master has already invented the scarecrow, so it can't be that. The feng shui master sits down in the field and closes his eyes. He listens. He doesn't know what for, but he'll know it when he finds it. He sniffs, searching for a smell that might give it away. Nope, he can't smell anything, but it was worth a try.

He shivers. It's the middle of summer, why is he cold? He opens his eyes and looks up, and sees that he's sitting in shadow. Suddenly, the feng shui master realises the problem. Farmer A and

Farmer B are on opposite slopes of a little hill. Farmer A's fields faces south, but Farmer B's fields face north. The sun rises in the east and sets in the west, but where is it at mid-day? Overhead? No, not overhead, not really. The sun spends more time in the southern part of the sky. If you're facing the south, you get more sunlight. If you're facing north, you'll get more shadow, because the hill behind you will get in the way.

The feng shui master has solved the problem. The south is a lucky place to plant crops. The north is unlucky. Another feng shui law has been formed, and soon the news travels around the neighborhood, and then the country. But "Chinese whispers" twist the scientific rationale. The original explanation is lost, and instead we are left with talk of good and bad luck. But the reasoning is perfectly sound.

Feng shui masters look, listen and

think. Then they come up with a theory and try it out. Eventually, the feng shui masters discover that some things work better than others and pass on the advice. Over the centuries, the advice of feng shui masters has been collected and passed on through family stories and old books. Magic and religion are forms of science, models to explain the way the universe works. And just like sciences, they are imperfect models. There is always something left unexplained, something which does not quite fit the laws drawn up by the thinkers of that religion, be they priests, witch doctors or particle physicists.

Some theories are disproved as human knowledge increases. Sensible people no longer believe that the world is flat, that the Earth is the center of the solar system or that the sun is pulled by a god in a giant chariot. But there are still some things that no-one can explain completely. One of the great unexplained things about the universe is death. Some of the earliest explanations for this phenomenon were provided in China, and because of the nature of the philosophy of the time, they drew their examples from the natural world: livestock, farming and marauders.

# THE WISDOM OF OLD AGE

As experts on crops and predictors of the weather, the early feng shui masters found themselves in an unenviable position. In the initial phases, they were probably treated just like trusted elders, old hands who would answer questions with the benefit of their long years, and much-respected members of the local community. Like the ship's pilot who can steer through the sandbanks without a second thought, these old men and women were the beneficiaries of experience, and their younger colleagues listened to them. In a world without books or writing to transmit information, bodies of knowledge depended on human luck and life to flourish.

Even in our own culture, the legends of

witchcraft share common themes. The toothless crone of medieval European lore is more than just a witch. Look deeper and we see other indicators. She is old, she is experienced, however she has lived her life, it is somehow appropriate because she has lived longer than anybody else. She has been in the village longer than anyone else can remember, and compared to her callow neighbors, she has a wealth of experience. This is the kind of person who, in the Far East, would find herself consulted on matters of feng shui.

She is probably the village midwife, because she has simply seen more births than anybody else. She has known and talked to more people in the course of her life, and so has a greater means of comparison. The younger folk in the village, tired of her endless warnings, and fearful that she is normally right, start to suspect that she has some kind of magic power. The ancient world was short on experts, and people who were unable to draw a line between natural and supernatural were liable to assume that someone who understood one would have equally ready answers for the other.

And so? And so the feng shui masters, who began as little more than weathermen and gardeners, over time become the prehistoric equivalents of priests and doctors. They are called upon to cure illnesses (at which some are irregularly successful, thanks to a knowledge of herbs). They are also called upon to ward off death (at which they are very bad, since death is a terminal affliction). When they fail and the patient dies, they are asked to explain themselves.

# QI: THE UNIVERSAL LIFE FORCE

❀

All cultures around the world ask themselves what is missing from a dead body. The ancient Egyptians claimed that the missing component was breath itself and their word "ka" mixed the concepts of breath and soul. So did the ancient Greek "psyche," and so did the ancient Chinese "qi." (It is pronounced "chee" to rhyme with "tea"). It's a nice, simple answer, but it creates more problems than it solves. It opens a whole new can of worms about where the qi goes when somebody dies. And if people have qi, does that mean that animals have qi as well? If animals have qi, doesn't that mean that they must have souls, and does that mean we shouldn't eat them?

Eventually the answers came back from

the feng shui masters. Yes, everybody has qi, but so does everything else. Every single thing in the world is possessed by the divine energy of qi, and it is this life force that binds us all together. Animals, vegetables and minerals all have qi, and it is quite safe for humans to eat anything with good qi in it. But qi, like any other living thing, can grow stale and decay. In the world of cookery, this maxim is easy to apply, since the fresher something is, the less decayed it is. But the feng shui masters were forced to apply this outside the world of cookery.

Qi, like the air itself, cannot be seen or held, but its presence can be felt. Living things have large amounts of qi, which leaves them when they die. Qi, like water, is kept freshest when it is constantly moving in slow swirls, and the idea of the curve became a fundamental principle in Chinese life. Roofs are curved to slow the passage of wind and water, and in the garden, paths are curved to move people in slow leisurely circuits. This keeps them calm and fresh, like water babbling along in a sunny brook. The alternative, a raging torrent through a straight gorge, was regarded as too forceful and exhausting.

This principle was also applied in the design of forts, where curving corridors make it difficult for approaching enemies to guess the number of defenders. They also made it difficult for them to build up a significant run-up to make a decent charge, thwarting invaders who wanted to batter through walls and doors.

The supernatural world has invaders of its own. Chinese lore talks of several different kinds of unearthly creatures, "yao," "mo," "gui" and "guai," sometimes translated vaguely as spirits, demons, devils and ghosts. These creatures have various different origins, but they all spell trouble for human beings. Some are simply elemental spirits who enjoy causing strife in the everyday world. Others are malignant ghosts of the dead, driven wild with anger because their descendants have not paid them the traditional forms of respect. Lost souls, creatures from hell and mischievous goblins, these creatures are feared all over the globe, but in China they are kept at bay by various methods in feng shui.

There are several charms you can place around your house, which are discussed later on. There are also many ways you can design your life and home to ward off these creatures. Because they travel in straight lines, they are deflected and confused by curves and barriers. They cannot hop over steps, so they can be kept out by bollards in doorways, hence the single doorstep found at the entrance to most Chinese temples.

Demons breed like insects in areas of stagnant qi, and so they can be shooed away by bright, happy environments. Noise can put them to flight, hence the

Chinese love of chimes and bells. During an eclipse, which the ancient Chinese believed was a creature trying to eat the sun, everyone would run outside banging gongs to scare it away again. In places of extreme haunting, only the loudest noise will do, and the Chinese resort to firecrackers.

Another form of haunting is that which is not brought about by demons, but by rotten or stagnant qi. Places with bad associations, such as old battlefields, locations where murders took place or the sites of anything unpleasant or unlucky, are thought to bring bad luck down upon the new residents. Chinese people moving house will check up on the previous owners, just to make sure that an apparent bargain does not actually involve paying a supernatural surcharge.

Still another way in which qi can go bad is when it is strangled or trapped. Rooms that do not receive regular airings, such as cellars and attics, are real breeding grounds for bad qi, but there are other influences that can bring it about in day-to-day life. Dirt itself will give off a supernatural stench of bad qi, and if easy movement is blocked in a house (by, for example, a cramped entranceway), the good qi will have trouble circulating, and will eventually go bad.

Your personal qi will also be upset by distractions. Low ceilings, overhanging beams and any objects that can catch at your clothing will constantly gnaw at your well-being. If you are always fretting about the precious vase on a rickety table, worrying about the expensive crockery falling off the shelves, or bending down to avoid a low doorway, these activities will take their toll, and eventually combine to leave you feeling on edge. Harmonious living includes making your own life easier. Having a house that invites you to be at peace and relax is a guaranteed way of increasing good qi, and your own sense of happiness.

The sharp jutting objects that might tear at your clothes or trip you up on the stairs can affect you even if they are outside the house. Just as feng shui discourages straight lines, it also advises you to avoid sharp corners and pointed objects. A building across the road with a sharp, pointed roof, a garden with a model cannon facing outwards at your front door, or even curtain rails with pointed ends will all conspire to keep you out of harmony.

Feng shui lore states that even if something reminds you of something else, it is as if that thing were really in the room with you. This can be a good thing, since, for example, a photograph of a happy time will be as if that happy time is always with you. But equally, if a spiral staircase resembles a corkscrew it will work like a drill between your luck and life, and should be avoided.

# RURAL FENG SHUI

Because feng shui began in the countryside, it still retains many vestiges of the
rural lifestyle. In theory, the best place for
feng shui living is in the country, in a
house that you've planned and built yourself, in a place that you chose yourself
with feng shui in mind. Cities didn't fit
the bill. For a long while, that was all
there was to feng shui lore on cities, but
times have changed.

Before we look at feng shui today, we
should discuss the various permutations
of rural feng shui, because it is the city's
failure to conform that makes feng shui
such a lucrative business in the urban
centers of the Far East. But it's still important to look at feng shui in its original
countryside setting if we're ever going to
understand how to apply it in the modern

world. And if you're one of those rare people who live in the countryside today, you're already very lucky in feng shui terms, because you're living in the world that feng shui was originally designed for.

Just as straight lines and pointed objects create bad qi, feng shui does not flourish in flat, unchanging places. There's nothing more boring to a feng shui sorcerer than flat land that just goes on forever. High ground is very important, because without hills, rivers have nowhere to flow, and a river without a course could mean an uncontrollable inundation, or simply no fresh water at all. Either way, an inability to control or access a water supply does not bode well for a rural community.

Without hill-tops you can never see far enough into the distance, both to watch for enemies and welcome friends coming to visit from distant places. There would also be nowhere to take refuge from floods, and since feng shui masters and farmers still required earthly protection from earthly dangers, nowhere for the warrior caste to build their hill-fort to watch over the entire community.

The feng shui can be very bad in flat, stagnant areas like parts of the Netherlands or the Mississippi delta, where the only breaks in the landscape are made by rivers which run above the level of the local land. Swampy areas are breeding grounds for mosquitos and disease, and the risk of flooding (a recurring theme in early feng shui) is so great as to make farming without modern protective measures almost impossible.

There are two enormous rivers in China, but they can be very unpredictable and have flooded many time in China's history. The people needed the water to drink and to nourish their crops, but they always lived in fear that they would wake up one day and find that they had to take a boat across the village because the water was waist-deep in the street. So hills are acceptable, because that decreases the risk of seeing your possessions float out the front door after heavy rain.

But, in typically Chinese fashion, the feng shui of hills states that you can have too much of a good thing. You should never build a house on the very top of a hill because that exposes it to the elements and is likely to cause trouble for your health because you have to spend more time huffing and puffing up the path every time you go home. Nor should you build your house beneath an overhanging rock or clifftop, because it is considered bad luck. In fact, you don't even have to be a feng shui master to see why. This partic-ular rule has nothing to do with demons or dragons, it's more concerned with falling rocks.

So the important thing about hills isn't that you stick your house on top of them, but that you should have plenty of them around to make for a nice view. Qi, like water, flows from the high ground towards the low, so if you're nestled in a nice valley you'll have plenty of water in the streams (important in early societies before western barbarians invented the faucet) and also lots of qi zipping around to bring you luck. As per usual, the valley should have an acceptable exit lower down, both to keep the qi from pooling and going stale, and the rainwater from slowly filling up the entire area and drowning the occupants.

The perfect feng shui location resembles an armchair. There is an imposing hill to the north to protect your house from the fierce north wind. Smaller hills flank it on either side like little arm-rests. If you are particularly lucky, you will have another even smaller hill like a footrest to the south, with a little freshwater stream running past it.

# WIND AND WATER

The crucial factor in feng shui building is maintaining harmony with the forces of nature. Mere mortals cannot compete with the immense natural forces that shape mountains, decide the courses of rivers, and cause lightning to strike and earthquakes to rumble. For this reason, feng shui masters are particularly keen on unimposing little cottages, set amidst bounteous gardens or protected by groves of trees.

We have already noted that "feng shui" means "wind and water," and it is the harnessing of these two forces that allows the best feng shui masters to gain better stores of qi. Hills or lines of trees will take the edge off the wind, changing it from harsh, unpleasant gusts to a warm, caressing breeze, in much the same way that a prism takes cold, white light and breaks it up into the colors of the rainbow. Water too is an important provider of qi. But you don't want the forceful rush of a whitewater river crashing past your home; you want the slow, leisurely meanderings of a calm stream. Where water pools and circulates, so does good qi.

Water is regarded as particularly important in Hong Kong, because there "water" and "wealth" are considered to be one and the same. Hong Kong was the natural place for this idea to arise because the harbor is the source of wealth for the people of Hong Kong. Hong Kong has no natural resources except its position and its people. It is not even self-sufficient in drinking water, and has to pipe it in from the mainland. What Hong Kong does have is an incredible harbor, shaped, as the feng shui masters unerringly point out, almost exactly like a huge money bag.

As the gateway to Asia, it is one of the biggest ports in the world, and its trade has flourished.

Are the feng shui masters pointing out Hong Kong's fortunate aspects with twenty-twenty hindsight, because there are a lot of people living in the city who would like to be told they made the right decision? Or are we being too harsh on what is essentially a polite, old-fashioned statement of the obvious. Forget the fortune-bestowing Nine Dragon hills (Kow Loon) twisting above the harbor, and concentrate instead on the explanation of the city's wealth. It is the port and harbor of Hong Kong that are the undeniable sources of its wealth, combined with the fiery will of the inhabitants to work hard for a better life.

# URBAN FENG SHUI

Feng shui has had to duck and dive through many adaptations over the years, but none so major as its application to living in large cities. Feng shui began as a rural, agrarian way of looking at the world, and initially concerned itself chiefly with the worries of ancient farming communities. But many people now live crowded in a single area, and this was bound to alter the original laws behind feng shui.

The simple answer is that living in a city is very bad news. Everybody else has their own problems and concerns that will rub off onto your own fortune, beautiful natural phenomena are eaten up by the ever-growing sprawl, and there are simply too many people in too small a place. This was precisely what the early feng shui masters said, although as progress marched on, they were forced by circumstances to adapt the old rules. After many years of wrangling, some feng shui masters grudgingly admitted that perhaps there were benefits to city life. Small, negligible bonuses like plumbing, sanitation and civic amenties. Nonetheless, they said, you still had to take care.

The rules of countryside feng shui still apply in the big towns and cities, but there are other problems. Urban roads are far less likely to be curved, and tend to zip backwards and forwards in straight lines. If your house is beside one of these straight roads, the good and bad should balance because both good and bad qi will simply charge past your door without stopping. If you have a front garden, do your best to make sure it is a green and pleasant place, because the slower, more leisurely clumps of good qi will be tempted to hover around you. As for the bad qi, who cares? Just let it keep on going.

# Street Life

Possibly the best place you can hope to live in a built-up area is in the middle of a large park (unlikely unless you are a forest ranger) or in a cul-de-sac. Good qi loves cul-de-sacs. To lucky spirits, a cul-de-sac resembles a little pool of calm amid the bustle of a city. Traffic rarely troubles a cul-de-sac because it's impossible to drive through it. You only drive into a cul-de-sac if you belong there. Another great thing about cul-de-sacs is that they are shaped like money bags. They store good qi, and with it luck and the chances to become wealthy.

# Dead Ends

**※**

However, there's a difference between a cul-de-sac and a dead end. If your street just suddenly stops in the middle of nowhere, this will bring very bad luck to whoever lives in the last house in the row. The bad qi running in a straight line will smack into the end of the street and begin to pool up. The pool will eventually calm the bad qi down and transform it into good qi, but not before a few spikes of frustrated bad spirits have tried to shoot off in straight lines looking for somewhere else to go. If your front door is in their path, you'll get far more than your fair share of bad luck unless you've taken steps to hold off their progress.

# T-Junctions

You will be in much deeper trouble if your house faces a straight street, for example, if it is on a T-junction. Cars will charge down the street and turn away before they smack into your garden wall, but demons are not so smart. If your door, gate or driveway directly faces the street that leads into the T-junction, this will be particularly tempting for bad luck. For more information, see under Junctions in the chapter titled The View From Your Window.

## Buckingham Palace

When the Queen of England is in London, she lives at Buckingham Palace. It has absolutely abysmal feng shui, because it's been built facing a huge, long wide avenue that collects bad qi up from as far away as Trafalgar Square and throws it full-force right against the palace gates. Luckily for the British monarchy, there is a statue in the middle of a roundabout right in front of the gates, which just about deflects most of the bad qi. Still, it's a very close call. The Queen is much better off when she is living in the country, but then again, a feng shui master would say that, wouldn't he?

## In the Shadows

Bad qi in the city can also be created by stationary objects like buildings. Have you ever been in a forest of very tall trees? The branches overhead from the tallest trees will soak up all the sunlight and goodness from above. Smaller plants have less of a chance to grow, and the forest floor is often bare but for the large trunks at the bases of the big trees. For the same reason, try to avoid living in the shadow of tall buildings, because they will soak up all the good qi before it gets to you.

# Falling Objects

🐝

There is also a considerable chance that demons will fall on your house from above. It only takes one feng shui master on the eighteenth floor to banish evil from his house, and for all you know it will come tumbling down into your garden. If you do find yourself dwelling in an area where this seems dangerous, ensure that any demons in your house or garden will have an easy exit like an open slat window or a small gap somewhere in the fence. Otherwise, they may stay around to cause trouble.

# Slices of Bad Luck

Watch out for sharp corners of buildings. If they are pointed at your house, they will be shooting bad qi at you. In a street of typical, western-style buildings, it's possible to find yourself running a gauntlet of bad qi, shooting at you from all areas. If some of the buildings are glassy skyscrapers, they may also be bouncing bad qi off their walls and back at each other again. It will be a kaleido-scope of catastrophe. However, in its favor, it's possible to argue that the average business district is well lit, and the more lights you see, the better the area's feng shui will be.

# Knife Edges

※

There's a shiny new business district in the north of Taipei, where a lot of the tower blocks have what appear at first glance to be very strange shapes. Many are not square at all, but irregular, and occasionally with rounded corners. This is to prevent the various businesses getting into escalating wars about who's firing bad qi at whom. You probably won't be lucky enough to live in such a considerate area (in fact, you would have to be a multinational corporation yourself before you could afford the rent) so look out for sharp corners from buildings, multi-story car parks or shop fronts that may be pointing at your house.

# Pei's Perils

࿓

One of my favorite buildings in this
Taipei business district was designed by a
famous Chinese architect, I.M. Pei, with
feng shui in mind. It has a rounded,
flowing shape, uplifted upper floors that
encourage continued success for the
occupants, and even protective spirits
built into the foyer as guardian statues.
But Pei's company came under fire in
Hong Kong over another of his buildings,
because when it comes to feng shui you
can always guarantee that someone will
not agree with your ideas.

Pei was asked to design a tower block
to house the Bank of China, and deliber-
ately set out to organize the best feng shui
arrangements he could. The site was in a
lucky location facing Hong Kong harbor,
but it was also a busy area surrounded
with bustling streets and sharp-edged

buildings. Pei designed extensive gardens with shrubs, trees and pools to deflect the bad qi of the nearby streets. He also made the building seventy floors high, the tallest in Hong Kong, so that no other building could dwarf it. Also, the walls of the building were all glass, letting sunlight in and coincidentally functioning as gigantic demon-warding mirrors.

Perfect ... except that others were not so sure. Don't forget that this building was designed to house the Bank of *China*, at a time when China would soon be taking control of the colony back from the British. Some critics found the feng shui of Pei's building very worrying, because they thought its sharp, tapering top made it look like a dagger pointing at the heart of Hong Kong, which would make for very bad qi indeed. It's one of the major problems with feng shui, some-times you just can't win.

# THE FIVE ELEMENTS

Feng shui may appear to be complicated, but is in actuality very simple. Areas of human habitation must be harmonized with their environment, and this is accomplished through the removal of any bad qi, the balancing of the five elements, and the use of the various influences and charms brought by the different points of the compass.

The elements in Chinese thought are the fundamental building blocks of both nature and good fortune. They are not just important as building materials, but also as colors, since each color in your room will represent a different element. No one element should be too strong in your home, unless you yourself are lacking in it. This chapter will tell you how each element affects your life and attitude. If you think you could do with more, or less, of each aspect in your life, all you need is pictures, wallpaper, paint or even throw cushions to increase a certain color's presence.

# Fire

A mystic energy because it is such a unique phenomenon, fire is represented by the color red. Fire is a symbol of growth and passion, of hunger for change and swift action. Too much of the Fire element in your feng shui (bright red walls, for example, with no mitigating elements) will make you quick-tempered and greedy, likely to burn up the friendship of others in your desire to get ahead. Too little will leave you listless and unco-operative, lazy and acquiescent. There will be no get-up-and-go in your life, and your fortune will be as much use as a damp squib. Fire can be balanced and controlled by the colors, symbols or presence of the element Water.

# Water

A ubiquitous item that exists in so many forms, from steam to ice, we cannot live without water. Represented by the colors black and blue (black for very deep water, and hence more powerful), Water is a symbol of calm and intelligence. It flows to fill its container, and is an excellent element in feng shui for encouraging sensitivity and thoughtfulness. Too much Water in your feng shui will make you tempestuous and unfathomable, easily wounded by the slightest comment or perceived gossip. Too little will leave you dry and unapproachable, thoughtless and acid-tongued. Water can be balanced and controlled by the element Earth, which soaks up its influence like hungry soil.

# Wood

The element behind all plants, not merely trees, Wood is another symbol of growth, although unlike Fire, it is slower and surer. Represented by the color green, Wood is a symbol of natural, sustained growth, and quiet confidence in one's abilities to triumph over all comers. Since roots and branches can wear down foundations where brute force would fail, Wood is an excellent influence for the success of long-term projects. Too much Wood will bring hangers-on determined to chop down your fortune and use it for themselves, and you will be too hard-headed to notice. Too little and you will be bent like a sapling. Wood can be balanced and controlled by the element Metal, which can keep it pruned.

# Metal

To the ancient Chinese, metal was magical because it seemed unbreakable. It is the material of plowshares and swords, but also of money, and so metal is a great influence at encouraging material wealth. Represented by golds, silvers and whites, Metal is a symbol of success and armor. Metal will make you incisive and decisive, but too much will make you sharp-tongued and miserly. It may also hold you like an anchor, even when you want to sail away. Too little Metal in your life may cause monetary riches to pass you by (Metal draws more Metal like a magnet). Metal can be balanced and controlled by Fire, which can alter and shape it in a furnace.

# Earth

The source of vegetation and hence food and life itself, Earth gives us fuel for fires and ore for metal. Represented by browns and yellows, and also by artefacts of glass or crystal, since they too come from the ground. Earth is a symbol of majesty and confidence, and also of reliability, since others can expect to benefit from your strength of will. Too much may make you slow and dull. Too little will leave you easily worried and hard to please, and probably unable to settle in any place for very long. Earth can be balanced and controlled by Wood, because only the roots of trees can undermine its strength and density.

# Shapes

Certain shapes are also regarded as symbols of the elements. Triangles symbolize Fire; curved, flowing objects stand in for Water; rectangular objects symbolize Wood; and trapezoids (like truncated triangles) represent the Earth. Metal objects are symbolized by the shape of an old Chinese ingot, which looks like a cross-section of a loaf of bread, with a square base but a domed top. The presence of these shapes in a room, house or garden are taken by feng shui masters to be exactly the same as the physical presence of the element itself. So remember that even a simple shape may be influencing your attitude or moods by exerting an elemental influence.

## Balancing the Elements

Everything in the universe contains greater or lesser amounts of the five elements. The feng shui of your home interior is composed chiefly of the materials of the five elements, as well as their symbolic presence. A wall is made of Earth (bricks), but a white wall is made of Earth and Metal (the color white). A white wall with a picture of the sea on it is made of Earth, Metal and Water. Each element has its particular strengths and weaknesses, and their uses along with particular objects in particular areas will be covered later.

# YOUR RULING
# ELEMENTS

There is one final object in a room which is ruled by the elements, and that is you yourself. Everyone is born in a year ruled by an animal of the Chinese zodiac (for particular details, see Animals and Pets), and each of these creatures is particularly strong in a particular element.

Each Chinese year also has its own element, providing two influences (or one very strong one) for the year of your birth. To find out the element and animal that is strong for both you and the general times, check the tables on the next pages. Remember, your ruling elements will be the ones you already possess. Perhaps you will want to accentuate them, or maybe calm them down by using their opposites in your decoration.

| Year Commencing | Year's Element | Year of the ... | Animal's Element |
|---|---|---|---|
| 6/2/1951 | Metal | Rabbit | Wood |
| 27/1/52 | Water | Dragon | Earth |
| 14/2/53 | Water | Snake | Fire |
| 3/2/54 | Wood | Horse | Fire |
| 24/1/55 | Wood | Sheep | Earth |
| 12/2/56 | Fire | Monkey | Metal |
| 31/1/57 | Fire | Rooster | Metal |
| 18/2/58 | Earth | Dog | Earth |
| 8/2/59 | Earth | Pig | Water |
| 28/1/60 | Metal | Rat | Water |
| 15/2/61 | Metal | Ox | Earth |
| 5/2/62 | Water | Tiger | Wood |
| 25/1/63 | Water | Rabbit | Wood |
| 13/2/64 | Wood | Dragon | Earth |
| 2/2/65 | Wood | Snake | Fire |
| 21/1/66 | Fire | Horse | Fire |
| 9/2/67 | Fire | Sheep | Earth |
| 30/1/68 | Earth | Monkey | Metal |
| 17/2/69 | Earth | Rooster | Metal |
| 6/2/70 | Metal | Dog | Earth |

| Year Commencing | Year's Element | Year of the ... | Animal's Element |
|---|---|---|---|
| 27/1/71 | Metal | Pig | Water |
| 15/2/72 | Water | Rat | Water |
| 3/2/73 | Water | Ox | Earth |
| 23/1/74 | Wood | Tiger | Wood |
| 11/2/75 | Wood | Rabbit | Wood |
| 31/1/76 | Fire | Dragon | Earth |
| 18/2/77 | Fire | Snake | Fire |
| 7/2/78 | Earth | Horse | Fire |
| 9/2/79 | Earth | Sheep | Earth |
| 16/2/80 | Metal | Monkey | Metal |
| 5/2/81 | Metal | Rooster | Metal |
| 25/1/82 | Water | Dog | Earth |
| 13/2/83 | Water | Pig | Water |
| 2/2/84 | Wood | Rat | Water |
| 20/2/85 | Wood | Ox | Earth |
| 9/2/86 | Fire | Tiger | Wood |
| 29/1/87 | Fire | Rabbit | Wood |
| 17/2/88 | Earth | Dragon | Earth |
| 6/2/89 | Earth | Snake | Fire |
| 27/1/90 | Metal | Horse | Fire |

| Year Commencing | Year's Element | Year of the ... | Animal's Element |
|---|---|---|---|
| 15/2/91 | Metal | Sheep | Earth |
| 4/2/92 | Water | Monkey | Metal |
| 23/1/93 | Water | Rooster | Metal |
| 10/2/94 | Wood | Dog | Earth |
| 31/1/95 | Wood | Pig | Water |
| 19/2/96 | Fire | Rat | Water |
| 7/2/97 | Fire | Ox | Earth |
| 28/1/98 | Earth | Tiger | Wood |
| 16/2/99 | Earth | Rabbit | Wood |
| 5/2/2000 | Metal | Dragon | Earth |
| 24/1/01 | Metal | Snake | Fire |
| 12/2/02 | Water | Horse | Fire |
| 1/2/03 | Water | Sheep | Earth |
| 22/1/04 | Wood | Monkey | Metal |
| 9/2/05 | Wood | Rooster | Metal |
| 29/1/06 | Fire | Dog | Earth |
| 18/1/07 | Fire | Pig | Water |
| 6/2/08 | Earth | Rat | Water |
| 26/1/09 | Earth | Ox | Earth |
| 14/2/10 | Metal | Tiger | Fire |

## Example: Balancing Elements

If you were born in 1976, the Chinese year's element is Fire. It is also the year of the Dragon, which is ruled by the Earth element. Both these elements will feature strongly in your character already, before you even think about your home. Perhaps a Metal or Water theme in your house (whites and blues) would keep you balanced. Green, as a representation of the Wood element, would also make a nice color scheme. Yellows or reds would only accentuate the elements that already exist in your character.

PART TWO

❈

# FENG SHUI
# IN PRACTICE

# INSIDE YOUR HOME

Each room in your house has certain special rules about placement and activity. There are various auspicious and inauspicious things that can be done with each room to maximize its potential. The placement of certain objects or symbols in certain sectors, will be covered in later chapters. But there are some aspects of your house's layout that have nothing to do with elements or lucky directions

# Bathroom

The traditional Oriental bathroom is very different from our own. It is, quite literally, a room with a bath in it and not merely a euphemism for a toilet, and the old style was for a huge, communal area where the whole household could soak and relax. The presence of the Water element makes the bathroom very auspicious, like a rejuvenating pond inside the walls of the house itself, but the plug hole is a symbolic exit from the house, and is best uncovered only when it is necessary to let the water out. Otherwise, luck (and money) might follow.

# Hall

The entrance hall is your welcome to the world, but also to yourself. Whatever is seen within it will be the first sight of your inner life that a visitor will receive, and so it is best kept tidy and attractive. A hall that runs straight through to the back door will let good luck straight out again, but a hall that is too cramped will require a mirror to double the space. A "welcome" mat is a good idea, as its message delivers a waft of friendly qi, and its presence allows visitors to show you respect by symbolically wiping their shoes before entering the house proper. In the Far East, visitors would remove their shoes completely.

# Lounge

Also known as a "living room," the lounge should be calming and planned with living in mind! A good lounge ensures that all the seats face each other to encourage conversation (if all chairs face the TV, it will encourage you to sit in front of it all day). It is also best kept separate from the dining area; if both activities have to take place in the same room, try symbolically walling off the table with a screen, lest your thoughts constantly dwell on food and not each other.

# Kitchen

The hearth was the center of any old-fashioned Chinese home, and the kitchen remains an important part of the home. Apartments without kitchens are like homes without hearths; the occupants will constantly strive for fulfilment, but are doomed never to find it until they move away. Kitchens are also likely to contain sinks and/or waste disposal facilities (see Bathroom above) but will also contain many sharp objects for use in cookery. Ensure that all sharp edges face away from the occupants (or are hidden entirely), in order to avoid accidents and adverse qi.

# Bedrooms

The bed should be placed in the yin sector of a room, or in other words, in the dark, quiet places away from the doors or windows. There should be no drafts or other distractions, and the occupants' feet should never point towards the door. This is because Chinese corpses are carried out of the house feet-first. Avoid overhanging beams or sharp corners that shoot bad qi at the sleeping occupant. If your luck has been bad, moving into a new house should also be a time for buying a new bed, as a symbol of a willingness to make a fresh start every morning, just as a new start has been made with the new dwelling.

# Dining Room

Try to avoid the mistake of having an ornate dining room, complete with expensive crockery, silverware and glasses. Dining is about eating food, not constantly fretting about the expensive china and whether the glasses have left marks on the precious table. If you want to impress your friends, serve them good food, not an obstacle course of breakable objects that will only distract both you and them from having a good time. See the chapter on Numbers for some suggestions about seating.

# Study

As more people work from their own houses, the home office is becoming a more common sight. Some form of symbolic separation from the rest of the house is advised, lest the study continually tempt you back for one last phone call before stopping for the day. If the study is on another floor, so much the better, but at the very least, the room should not be used for any other purpose or it *will* interfere with your home life. The same applies for studies belonging to scholars. The sight of all your books will encourage you, but the other distractions in the room will cancel out the benefits.

## Utility Rooms

Some houses isolate some important items, such as the washing machines and driers. As electrical objects, they will put out a lot of yang energy, not to mention noise, so ensure they are not too close to a sleeping area. They will also put out a lot of heat, and so the utility room should always be well ventilated.

# THE POINTS OF THE COMPASS

✽

Each point of the compass has its own meaning and resonance, and rules an aspect of your fortune. If the house is damaged or dirty in that area, your fortune will be too. Of course, the opposite applies too, and the right decoration can benefit that sector of your life.

Nobody knows exactly when the compass was invented in China. The first recorded use dates from the 1100s, but legends stretch back another two thousand years. The early Chinese compass looked significantly different from the version we all know. It was not shaped like a needle, but like a spoon, supposedly to reflect the shape of China itself. China's mountainous, rocky north was represented by the bulky, heavy end upon which the spoon-like compass spun. The flat, low-lying south was represented by the "handle," the lighter end which actually did the orienteering. For this reason, ancient Chinese maps have south at the top, because that is the direction in which the irregular-shaped compass would come to rest.

# North

To the ancient Chinese, the North was a dark, forbidding place, a bleak land of cold steppes and rocky tundra that led to unending wastes of ice. It was also the home of the Manchu warriors, the brutal tribe that swarmed across the Great Wall and made China their own. For everyday Chinese people, the North was a frontier land where anything could happen, and where a canny individual could come back rich and successful. For this reason, the North is the direction of Career, is said to hold the greatest sway over the young men and adult sons of a family. Its identifying color is black, and rules over the health of the room-owner's ears.

# North-east

The North-East was where Kublai Khan established his court when he became the ruler of China. Since the latter days of the Ming dynasty, it has been China's North Capital ("Bei-Jing"), and the seat of the Emperor's power. For any commoner in China, the only way to a career in the Imperial service was to pass difficult civil exams, held in the capital. For this reason, the North-East rules learning and self-improvement. The hand holds the brush that writes the exam, so the North-East rules the health of the hands and fingers. It is also the origin of the piercing Siberian wind, so is a bad choice for door placement.

# East

The East is the direction of the rising sun, and so this direction has become the Chinese symbol of springtime and renewal. It rules your family and health, and is associated with the color green and the striving element of wood. It also has particular resonance for the mature males of a family, since they are expected to rise with the dawn to tend to their chores. It has been a long time since most people lived by a farmer's work schedule, but this is a vestige that has lived on, especially in the Far East, where many office workers cram a study session into their "extra" hour between arriving at work and the beginning of the working day.

# South-East

As one might expect from the location of Hong Kong and the South-East Asian "tiger" economies, this is the direction of wealth. The South-East sector rules most aspects of the occupant's finances, and is a particularly good place for the entrance to a business, as long as it opens onto a street brimming with good qi. A South-Eastern door that opens onto an ugly scene, a drain, a fast river, or motorway is likely to wash away the owner's wealth. This direction is particularly important for the eldest daughter of the family, since a daughter's marriageability was often directly determined by the extent of the dowry her family could provide. For related reasons, the South-East rules the hips.

# South

In the northern hemisphere, south-facing slopes receive the most sunlight. The extra warmth and light has led the south to become the direction representing summer, and the bright hopes provided by the family's women, especially married daughters who may have left home. The South is often represented by the color red, not only because it is associated with the element Fire, but also because red is the color of a Chinese woman's wedding dress. The South is can be a particularly influential direction upon fame and rank (the South Capital or "Nan-Jing" was also a place where the talented could find great success). Since it is where the sun shines most, it is where glittering attainments shine best.

## South-West

Both the South-West and West are associated with marriage, because old Chinese marriages used to take place at sundown. The Chinese character for marriage still shows a woman, a man, and a sun low in the sky. For this reason, families should pay particular attention to the South-Western sector of their house during the days and weeks before a wedding. A negative influence here can ruin the big day. This direction also rules the internal organs, and is of particular importance for the mother of the family, since a mother's great achievement is to bring up her offspring to become good husbands and wives themselves.

# West

The final destination of the sun during its daily journey across the sky, and the direction of the mysterious, exotic lands of Europe. For traders on the silk road, the West was a travelogue of hardships, with mountains, bandits, deserts and steppes, but ultimate rewards of great riches. It is also the direction that rules the fates of children, where both parents and children alike face long years of work and hardship, in order to become balanced and rounded individuals. Children are also the ones that parents must rely upon in their twilight years, and the place of the setting sun is there to remind us all that as our descendants revere us, so must we respect them.

# North-West

The long trading routes out of China feature again in the ruling passions of the North-West, which is the direction of travel and aid from kind strangers. Chinese people were reminded by the works of Confucius to always "welcome guests from afar"; the North-West combines the idea of travel with an admonition to be kind to others, for who knows when you will need them to return the favor. This direction is of particular importance to the host who will entertain the guests, the father of the family or any other older men of the household.

# The Center

The compass has eight points, but it also has a center. While the walls and edges may bring influences upon a room, the center of the room is where it must function. As the "qi center," the middle of the room rules the occupant's general well-being. Whatever occupies the middle of a room is likely to be ever-present in the occupant's thoughts, and so it is vital that it is something that encourages good, rather than bad energies. Take particular care to ensure that sharp objects are kept away from the center of the room, otherwise a knife in the center of your dwelling may spike your fortune just as surely as a knife in your heart.

# COLORS AND TEXTURES

Colors are of great importance to feng shui, and not only because the color of surfaces and objects are a vital part of any kind of interior decorating. Modern scientists have proved that human beings are affected by the colors of their surroundings, but this is something that feng shui practitioners have known for centuries.

A fundamental problem with color in feng shui is that only half of the maxims and legends will relate directly to a non-Chinese person. Colors have their own, different significance in our culture, and you may wish to use discretion, rather than follow the letter of the Chinese law. As with many other aspects of feng shui, part of the lore is practical, based on similarities and associations that may remind the viewer of certain objects or states of mind. But there are also a number of pieces of color lore that stem from puns, which may not work if you do not speak Chinese.

# Black

Black is the color of night without stars or moon, the darkest moment of the night when all seems lost. It is also as dark and forbidding as the night can be before the coming of the dawn. It can thus be used as a symbol of a new beginning, and the end of a time of strife. In Chinese thought, black was often used as a symbol for water instead of the more usual blue, and can be used as a substitute for the element itself. Black rules the Northern compass point. It should be used sparingly in interior decoration as it is a yin color, and hence a depressing influence on the occupants.

# Blue

The more usual symbolic color of water in the West, the Chinese are more likely to describe it as the color of the sky. Blue rules the North-East and the South-East. It is a symbol of deep knowledge and spirituality, but also of changeability. The tides may come and go with deceptive regularity, but the nature of their arrival can never be predicted. Will the high tide tomorrow be a flood? Or will it be calm and tepid? Also a sign of faith and truthfulness; "true blue" is not a phrase only found in the West, for a blue sky has no clouds and no obstructions. Too much blue will make you indecisive and fickle.

# Brown

Brown is the color of earth and of clay, and is hence a symbol of steadfastness and reliability. Earth is the solid foundation upon which a house is built, and the element of Earth represents the fundamental foundations of somebody's character. As a paint color, if it is too dark it will create shadows and yin essence in the room. But light brown is also an inauspicious color, because it is the color of calling cards used during a period of mourning. A very problematic color if used in anything more than small amounts. But brown as the natural color of wood is acceptable, since that is a symbol of the Wood element.

# Copper

Copper is regarded in China as a mild form of gold, and so will bring the benefits of Metal with an extra, minor influence of wealth. It is also said to be an important component in the summoning of dragons; some believe that dragons enjoy it as a delicacy, others that they are attracted by its smell. These days it is rarely regarded as a suitable metal for adornment or decoration, but in feng shui it cannot fail to bring luck and good qi. Copper brings dragons and hence qi; a close approximation of its modern-day use for conducting electricity.

# Gold

It is unlikely that you will have too many solid gold objects lying around your home, indeed, it is unwise, as it is possible to have too much of a good thing. But as a gilt (on clocks, for example) or even just as a color, gold will have positive effects. As an example of the element Metal, gold is a very strong influence. It is also an obvious symbol of wealth, but should not be used to excess lest its owner become miserly and corrupt. The old imperial palace in Beijing lay at the feet of the Gold Hills, whose fortune-bearing waters would flow into the precincts, collect against the Emperor's dwelling, and wash its luck into the royal family.

# Green

Green has many meanings to the Chinese, confused still further by the Chinese language's own confusion with the color. Some Chinese "greens" are actually blue, a problem which probably began when someone defined green as the color of jade, without realizing that jade runs through a gamut of shades, including green and blue. Green is the color of Wood (the Wood element includes plants), and, in modern times, the color of the American dollar, and hence a symbol for money and wealth. Too much green in your decoration can turn you green with envy, and according to Chinese lore you may have good cause, since it is also a color associated with infidelity and adultery.

# Gray

Feng shui lore firmly believes in the unity of opposites. Black and white, yin and yang, light and dark: all these things must be balanced to create harmony. Since gray is neither black nor white, but a murky combination of the two, it is a symbol of occlusion and secrecy. Gray is the color of non-committal or anonymity, and is said to denote someone with something to hide. It is the color of spies and intrigue, but also of a wise politician, waiting in the wings to make his move. Good for anonymous suits or trenchcoats, but perhaps a little too bland for decoration.

# Iron

Since ancient times in the West, iron has been thought to repel the attacks of fairies and other forest spirits. In China, iron was thought to injure the eyes of dragons, and was used to ward off unfavorable influences. Too much of it about the home, of course, will also ward off any friendly dragons, along with the good qi they might have brought. It was occasionally used in Chinese weather spells, since iron and dirt thrown together into pools was thought to irritate dragons so much that they would burst free and create fierce storms in the sky. Even in ancient Chinese farming communities where rain was of vital importance, risking the wrath of dragons was discouraged.

# Orange

A multiplicity of meanings for this color. It is the color of the setting sun, and hence associated with gregarious activity like dining out or going to parties. A sign of sociability and *bonhomie*, though if used to excess it can tire you out, or even turn you into a herd animal with no sense of self. Thanks to the robes worn by some Buddhist sects, orange can be a symbol of striving for spiritual perfection. As a mixture of Fire (red) and Earth (yellow), it can be particularly effective in countering an excess of the Water element in your home. Orange the fruit, as opposed to orange the color, has a separate entry under Fruits and Flowers.

# Pearl

The lustrous, smooth qualities of pearl have combined over time to make it a symbol of the Moon in Chinese thought (see Silver). It is also associated with money, both through its use as a semi-precious object, and its origin in a shell (see Shells). The pearls in the sea are said to be guarded by dragons, which is perhaps an ancient reference to sharks writhing in the distance. It can also be a symbol of attainment in spite of hardships, or perhaps even because of them, because the production of a pearl requires the irritation of an oyster. While they are beautiful objects or textures, they may bring strife if used to excess.

# Red

Ancient Chinese had over a dozen kinds of "red," creating distinctions that are difficult to draw, even for modern Chinese people. But in general, it is representative of the element Fire, and also of good luck. Money and gifts are handed out in red envelopes at weddings, and the traditional Chinese wedding dress is a fiery red. Red is a very popular color in Chinese interior design, but normally for public buildings such as theaters, halls or temples. As the primary color in a room, it is nice to visit, but you wouldn't necessarily want to live there. Fiery red is useful for awakening energies, but take care its use to excess does not cause occupants to become hot-tempered and hyperactive.

# Silver

A symbol of the Metal element, and hence also of wealth, silver has many other properties in feng shui. As in many other religious traditions, silver is associated with the Moon, and in China the idea of moonlight has both a positive and negative side. The Moon does not shine with its own light, but is nonetheless beautiful, and so silver has come to represent success or beauty through the light of others. Musicians who require composers, actors who require playwrights, and any other kind of occupation that cannot shine without another's creative input, are all ruled by silver. Its use is to be avoided by those individualists who wish to go it alone.

# White

Represents purity and "yang" essence. White, like the white belt of a martial artist, is the color of innocence and inexperience, but not in a negative way. After all, if the novice martial artist is wearing the belt, they must be training to improve their skills. Also a symbol of the element Metal. White reflects light, making a room look bigger than it really is, and multiplying the output of lights, or the input from the windows. For this reason, it also functions in Chinese lore as a weak form of mirror, and it can be employed to offset mild problems in architectural feng shui, such as a slightly irregular room shape.

# Violet

Traditionally the color of a hermit's robes, violets, mauves, and purples are the hues associated with a driven individual, shutting themselves away from the world in order to pursue their great talents. A color of artistic or literary creation, and of passion, truth, and refusal to compromise. As a mixture of Fire (red) and Water (blue), it is an excellent color to use if you do not want to upset a room that is already perfectly balanced. Take care not to use it in great amounts; while it may encourage your creative talents, it could also turn you into an isolated eccentric.

# Yellow

A symbol of the element Earth because of the silt that gives the famous Yellow River its name, Yellow has come to represent the Emperor himself, and hence China as a whole. After a famous nineteenth-century incident in which the Emperor showed gratitude by wrapping a friend in his own Imperial yellow coat, a "Yellow Jacket" is the term reserved for a close family member or friend with unprecedented privilege and access. If used to excess, the occupant may not only suffer from the standard problems of too much Earth, but also from delusions of grandeur. A very pale yellow, almost indistinguishable from white, will also work as a very weak mirror for amplifying qi.

## Pastel Shades

Apart from light brown, which is associated with mourning, most lighter shades should be regarded as feng shui influences of diluted power. The various shades of off-white will bring a mild bonus with the shade, and a diluted bonus of the bright reflectivity of whiteness itself. Most people are more likely to use muted colors rather than bold primary hues, and this will mean that the element or feeling represented by the color is not quite so influential in the room's feng shui. Occupants with extremely strong elemental deficiencies may find that the opposite effect is more desirable, and that their fortune can be greatly improved by the selection of the right amount of a bright, distinctive color.

# Rough Textures

The most important aspects to look for when selecting textures is the play of light and shadow. Rough brickwork or a similarly harsh texture is not a problem, so long as the irregularities do not create shadows on the wall. Beware too of protrusions that can snag at the occupants' clothes as they pass by. Chinese floors vary, with ideal texture depending on the location of the house. Rough floor textures are more acceptable in the North, where the custom of removing shoes on entry is less common. Take care that your floor does not have protrusions that can trip or snag. It should be even, although creaking floorboards are not discouraged; these "singing boards" can deter intruders.

## Smooth Textures

It can never be stressed enough that one of feng shui's fundamental precepts is "all things in moderation." We should seek equilibrium in all things, and it is always possible to have too much of a good thing, no matter how good that thing may at first appear. Smooth walls are quite acceptable, so long as they are not so smooth that they cause glaring reflections for the lights in the room, and hence confuse and annoy the occupants. An even floor is common sense, but a floor that is too polished will have no place for the toes to grip, and may cause the occupants to lose their footing.

# FRUITS AND FLOWERS

✿

Many kinds of plant and flower have a particular significance in feng shui, whether they are used as building materials, decorations, or even as the subject matter of art and sculpture. Because feng shui lore emphasises a need to live in harmony with nature, the presence of plants is a very positive and healthy thing.

Dried or preserved plants are perfectly acceptable in the home. Fresh or living varieties will exert an even more powerful influence, but must be tended carefully. They may exert a better influence while alive and healthy, but if they become diseased or rotten they will start to have a negative effect. As with the other aspects of feng shui, some of these symbols are obvious, and others are rooted in old Chinese folktales.

# Large Plants

Particularly large plants are not only used for the symbolism they bring or the psychological attitudes they can inspire. They are also powerful, living embodiments of the Wood element, a fact which may influence the colors you use for the room in which they sit. A room already heavy with Wood colors may not benefit from the installation of a plant as much as one with an excess of one of the other elements. Plants are also very useful for softening the sharp corners and angles of rooms, and thus reducing the "daggers" and "arrows" of bad qi.

# Flowers

Revered world-wide for their power to cheer the down-at-heart, all flowers bring brightness and joy into the home, although the essence of good qi will only last for as long as the flowers themselves do not wilt. Flowers should be kept fresh and watered, and removed as soon as they show signs of ill health. Dried flowers, plastic flowers or artistic representations of flowers are all acceptable, but will never fully live up to the promise and perfume of the real thing. The one advantage they do possess is that you need never worry about forgetting to water them and causing an outbreak of bad qi. Several types of flower have special powers of their own, listed separately below.

# Bamboo

Famously flexible and enduring, bamboo is a symbol of an ability to move with the times and bend with the prevailing wind. Bamboo groves are said to be haunted at night (which is actually the keening sound made by the touching stems as the wind blows between them). Consequently, a little bamboo brought into the house can "vaccinate" the house from invasion by evil spirits. Chinese bamboo flutes are particularly common in feng shui locations, because the playing of a flute will soothe the tired spirit. When tied with red cord and hung at angles to each other, a pair of flutes can counteract the effects of overhanging beams and sharp corners by "rounding off" the walls or ceiling.

# Cherry

With its bright red color and sweet taste, the cherry is a symbol of youthful vigor, especially in matters of the heart, where in the S it will keep the family's maidens young and fresh, in the NE it will encourage the young men of the family to strive for betterment. But it is not merely the cherry's fruit that exerts an influence in feng shui; the tree itself has become a powerful symbol through the poetic associations evoked by its blossoms. The beautiful, almost translucent flowers with an eerie glow were associated for a long time with magic and lunacy. Recently, they have symbolized youthful sacrifice, especially in Japan where they were the emblem of the kamikaze pilots.

# Chestnuts

The chestnut is an aphrodisiac, and its powers are especially strong in encouraging the man of the household to produce children. If the image of the chestnut is placed in the Children (W) sector it will work as a charm to encourage male potency. If placed in the Marriage sector (SW) it will encourage a second honeymoon of wedded, or more appropriately, bedded bliss. If placed in the Children (W) sector it will have the same effect, but is also more likely to bring fertility in the lady of the house, and the promise of pregnancy. The color chestnut does not have the same powers, since in Chinese it is not called "chestnut" but the less-poetic "red-and-sack-brown".

# Cypress

The cypress tree, like the pine, remains green in winter, and is a symbol of endurance and calm in the midst of strife. Objects made from the tree are symbols of the Wood element, especially powerful in encouraging concentration and calm during times of hardship. If placed in the Knowledge sector they will encourage study, if placed in the Children sector they will prove to be a positive influence on fertility. When all your acquaintances seem turned against you, placing cypress objects in the NW sector will encourage your true friends to take a stand by your side.

# Ivy

A Chinese poet once sang of the creation goddess of the hills, who came "girdled with ivy". This strong and resilient plant, notorious for climbing walls and fences, is an extremely useful plant in feng shui for integrating man-made objects with the natural world. In East Asia, some large buildings even use it indoors as adornment for the foyer fountains, to bring the natural world physically inside the building. Ivy, and other kinds of "creeping" plants, are also useful in the grounds or garden, particularly in softening the lines of chain fences and brick walls. Beware the poison variety; your feng shui will be disturbed if you have an allergic reaction to your own house or garden!

# Lotus

Beloved of the Buddha, the lotus is a beautiful flower that blooms in swamps and muddy pools. It is a symbol of creation and of renewal, and of the search for enlightenment. In feng shui, a lotus can be a symbol of triumph over adversity, as beauty struggles and succeeds in releasing itself from the confines of its environment. Placed in the NW, a lotus will encourage occupants to fly the nest and seek their fortune. In the SW it encourages quarrelling couples to settle their differences and fall in love all over again. In the N, NE, S, or SE, it encourages the occupant to aim high and strive for great achievement in career, study, fame, or finance respectively.

# Magnolia

※

The magnolia charms and beguiles, basically a positive influence in feng shui, although it is open to abuse. It can influence the occupant to impress others with approachability and sweetness, but those who employ its powers must remember others should like them for more than the way they look. The magnolia will bring fame and fortune in the S or SE, but purely for its own sake. It should be carefully combined with other influences to ensure that the occupant's talents are worth the attention. If used as the sole influence in matters of the heart (place it in the SW), it comes fraught with danger, for who wants to choose a spouse purely on looks?

# Orchid

A combination of rarity, uniqueness, strangeness, and exclusivity makes the orchid the flower symbolizing good taste and high-class romance. But the orchid's influence is like a rare and strong spice: if used to excess it will fail. Too many orchid influences in the NE will turn the occupant into a snob, seeking only the strangest and most exclusive pursuits, and looking down upon one-time friends. If employed in the S sector it will bring many suitors to the young ladies of the family, although it is no guarantee that their intentions are honorable. If used in the SW it will bring a husband of rare breeding, but take care he does not mistake you for another temporary curiosity.

# Peaches

The peach is the fruit of the celestial emperor, and grows in the gardens of heaven. The Monkey King sneaked into the gardens of heaven and stole some peaches for himself. When he ate them, he was granted immortality, and the peach is said to confer long life on any who eat enough of them. In times of illness, the peach can protect the old men of the family if placed in the NW, the old women of the family in the SW. In the N sector, it discourages early retirement, in the SE it guarantees a long and prosperous income. If placed in the SW of a honeymoon couple's new home, it creates a long and loving marriage.

# Pear

Because the pear tree has a long and fruitful lifespan, the pear is another symbol of long life. Pear emblems can be used like peaches (see above), and are influential in the W for those who want many children, and the N for a productive and munificent career. The "Pear Garden" was a famous Tang dynasty drama school, and "Pupils of the Pear Garden" is an old name for actors. If you seek a career on the stage or screen, try adding pears and pear emblems to your feng shui, especially in the S (fame) sector. Unless you want to be an actor or lawyer, keep pears away from the NE, where they encourage falsehood in your academic work.

# Peony

The peony is associated in Chinese folk-lore with wise counsel and statesmanship, and is known as the "King of Flowers". If placed in the SW it will bring luck in love. If placed in the SE it will bring great financial success. In the N it will bring a working life that seems to consist of nothing but promotion after promotion, and a trusted and respected position within the company or organization. If placed in the S it will bring the occupant great fame. If the occupant is suffering from poverty, demotion or infamy, check the same sectors for wilted peonies, damaged peony emblems or any other sign that may have caused the occupant's decline in good fortune.

# Pine

The pine tree flourishes even during the cold winter months, and so is regarded all round the world as a symbol of renewal and the promise of spring. According to Chinese folklore, if you can find a pine that is three thousand years old or more, you should be able to find a lump of resin underneath the bark that is shaped like a dragon. If you can find and eat ten pounds in weight of such resin, you will live for five hundred years. Said to be a symbol of faithful marriage (because pines are supposed to grow in pairs). A lone pine is a symbol of unrequited love. Otherwise use pine emblems like those of the cypress tree.

# Plum

The plum tree is commonly found in Chinese art as an old and gnarled creation, clearly of great age, but still producing flowers and fruit. A symbol of prosperous life and immortality, it is also, thanks to a pun in Chinese, a symbol of grace and beauty. Most influential when placed in the E sector, where it will guarantee long and healthy lives to members of the family. Take care not to place it in the N sector, since it brings success in later years, and the young men of the family may not wish to have to wait so long for rewards and prosperity. Ageing couples without children may benefit from plum emblems in the W sector.

# Pomegranate

This fruit is bursting with seeds, and has become a symbol of plenty. It is a very powerful influence indeed when placed in the E or W sectors, since it is said to bring vast returns on investment, and is particularly strong when bringing good qi to the occupants' prospects for fertility. Families hoping to keep numbers down would be wise to check there are no pomegranate symbols either in the relevant sections, or visible through the windows. If placed in the SE sector it will bring great bonuses of wealth, interest on investments, and repayments of insurance. If placed in the N or S it may make the occupant a strong and respected leader, with many loyal followers.

# Rose

A symbol of romantic love in the West, the rose now has the same meaning in the Far East. But every rose has its thorn, for love can bring anguish and injury to the heart. Often given as a token of love, you should take care to give an auspicious rather than an inauspicious number (see Numbers). Signs of love and happiness when used in the W and SW, but have deceptive powers elsewhere. If placed anywhere except these two sectors, it may bring apparent good fortune to the occupants, but with hidden strings attached. The feng shui composition of the rest of the area will determine whether or not those strings will be acceptable to the occupant.

# Willow

In North-East Asia, the willow tree was used in religious ceremonies. A kind of tea was prepared from its bark which induced a trance-like state in whoever drank it. It has thus become a symbol of intoxication and of the power of divination, since it is told that those who drank of the willow tea could see into the future for a brief period. As in the west, the "weeping" willow is a symbol of sadness and endurance, especially in matters of the heart. It should be used carefully in feng shui to avoid bad fortune in love.

# FURNITURE AND OBJECTS

❀

Beyond the walls, windows, colors and textures of a room, we still have to consider the actual objects that go inside it. Some are unique to the Far East, some are everyday objects all around the world, but all of them can influence the general fortune and feng shui of your house.

Don't forget that the colors and materials of the objects will also bring influences of their own, a Metal chair and a Wooden chair are quite different, and their effects will depend on the elemental composition of the rest of the room. As usual, the wise feng shui decorator should always seek to achieve balance, and the variation of objects and artefacts can make all the difference.

# Heavy Objects

Sturdy tables, stone statues or heavy desks will add balance and security. If your job prospects are looking unsafe at the office, try moving your desk to the N sector. If your children are proving unruly, perhaps a heavy object in the W sector will slow them down. If you and your spouse are quarrelling, perhaps a statue in the SW will help, especially if it is an animal associated with calm or fidelity (see Animals and Pets). Heavy objects in a strong sector may make the occupant sluggish or lethargic, so examine their placement carefully. In the case of statues, remember that the statue is a heavy example of both the subject, and of the material from which it is made.

# Amber

Represents the soul of the tiger, left behind after the earthly creature's death. It is thus a powerful charm for those born in the Year of the Tiger and a powerful ward against bad fortune. In the E sector it can protect the family from illness, in the central sector it can protect a home from thieves and intruders. As a representation of the tiger, amber is imbued with the element Wood. Thanks to its warm coloring, it is also a talisman of the element Fire, and this should be borne in mind if it is placed in a room that already has a surfeit of one or both of these elements.

# Ancestors

The family in Chinese life is very different from the modern Western variety. In the everyday world, one is considered to be related to, beholden to, and obligated to anyone linked by up to seven generations or ties, and this extends laterally as well as vertically. Your grandparents are separated from you by two links, your children by one, their spouses by two and their spouse's parents by three. Obligations remain beyond death, and the tending of graves is one of your duties. You should also involve your ancestors in family occasions by placing their pictures somewhere prominent. They in turn will intercede on your behalf in the spirit world, and may be able to influence your good fortune.

# Bells

There is something quite magical about the ringing of a bell. Metal, let us not forget, is the last of the five elements to have been harnessed by the ancients, and the resonations of a bell or gong are thought by many cultures to echo in the land of the gods. When a bell chimes, it opens a line of communication to heaven, and is hence good fortune. Bells are also used on shop doors to warn the owner of the arrival of new customers. The mere presence of a bell near an entranceway is said to act as a deterrent to thieves. This applies equally to places of business and private residences.

# Books

🙘

Literature and writing of any kind are all signs of learning and wisdom. Chinese writing looks so good that it is often used as decoration in itself, but always make sure you know what something says. Every single piece of writing on your walls will function as a constant reminder: all well and good if it is wishing you luck, but what if it is less fortunate? Books are stored knowledge, of course, and work as reminders to study and improve oneself. Holy books exude a protection from evil spirits. Unseemly books may encourage unseemly fates, especially since many first-time guests will find themselves perusing your bookshelves for clues about your character.

# Celebrity Portraits

Pictures of celebrities and famous people have always been popular, especially among the young, but their value in feng shui is problematic. When it comes to those who portray fictional characters, the potential fortune can be mixed. When a celebrity's portrait is part of the feng shui of a room, the occupants must ask themselves carefully what they are hoping for. Do they want the actor's fortune in a particular sector? Or do they want the character's fortune? Does a fan wish for the actor's attention (unlikely), that of someone like him (possible), or someone like the character he plays? What if he plays the villain …? Take care, especially in the Wealth (actor's or character's?) and Marriage sectors.

# Coral

Coral was said to be the underwater tree of a great goddess, and was regarded by the Chinese as an inexplicably magic object. Although clearly a growing object (some feng shui manuals would rather file it under "Fruits and Flowers"), when touched it can turn as hard as stone. This has made it a symbol of transformation and mystery, loved as much for its strange behavior as for its bright colors. The Buddhist Paradise has giant coral trees, and pieces of coral in the study (NE) sector will bring a sea-change of improvement. In the Marriage (SW) sector it can add a little zing to a relationship, and remind the lovers how lucky they are to have each other.

# Chairs

※

The nature of a chair will have a great deal of influence on the person who sits in it. Reclining chairs may relax the occupant, but will also encourage lethargy. Chairs with high backs and small bases will keep the occupant alert, but also tense. Remember to ensure that chairs support the occupant and encourage the demeanor for which they are intended. Work chairs should not encourage slouch or sloth, and chairs in the dining room should make eating a pleasurable experience. The number of chairs in a room or around a table can have implications of its own, and should be monitored carefully to ensure the best fortune. See the chapter on Numbers.

# Chopsticks

Should never be left sticking upright out of a bowl, since then they resemble incense offerings left for the dead. In classical Chinese they are called "helpers" because they aid the eating process. A chance pun has led them to be referred to as "hasteners," and their presence in a particular sector may speed up developments. Place in the N sector to speed up promotional prospects, in the NE to aid studies and in the NW to enable a speedy return for travelers. Japanese chopsticks have pointed ends, which are less favorable because they create sharp and adverse qi. Chopsticks should always be kept in pairs: an odd number signifies that something is missing or otherwise at fault.

# Door

A crucial part of the feng shui of any room or house. The view upon entering or exiting through a door is a vital influence upon the mind and fortune of the occupant; an auspicious sight is good news, and, conversely, a vista of ugliness will slowly corrupt one's good fortune. The door is also the primary point of entry for good qi, and should not be blocked by pillars or other obstructions. Check under the Points of the Compass to see which sector your door is in. The ruling sector in which the door is placed (e.g. career, marriage, health) will be directly affected by the door's auspicious or inauspicious location.

# Electrical Objects

As an energy force, electricity is a modern manifestation of qi. Because electrical objects use energy for positive purposes, they are yang influences, but may dry up a room's qi and overload the senses of the occupants if turned up too bright, played too loud, or too often. All electrical objects come under this umbrella, although washing machines and refrigerators are more balanced (containing both yin water and yang heat, or yang electricity and yin cold). Cookers and heaters in particular are best placed in yin areas for the sake of balance. Take care that televisions and gaming consoles are not placed like idols, or they will be worshipped. Books around a computer will encourage its use for education and study.

# Fountains

🏶

The gentle trickle of water is renowned
for soothing the troubled brow, and fountains are good objects for encouraging
calm. In public meeting places, they
encourage the return of distant travelers,
especially if the traveler in question can
be encouraged to throw a coin into the
waters. In business premises, the fountain
is influential in bringing cash, especially
in restaurants, where it works as a fine
conversation piece. Although you are
unlikely to have an indoor fountain, one
in your garden will still influence your
feng shui. Place it in the SW for a
trouble-free marriage, in the E for an
easy home life, and in the NW for long
journeys without strife.

# Hanging Objects

Hanging objects work like plants, since they are free-floating objects that soften the harsh corners of a room, and aid the circulation of slow-moving, positively-charged qi. Mobiles, wind chimes, and similar suspended objects are useful for placing components in a part of the room without taking up unnecessary floor or wall space, but take care that the hangings do not swing too low and disturb the occupants. The soothing tinkle of wind-chimes in your marriage sector may well calm marital disagreements, but not if both parties keep on walking into them. Outside the house, wind-chimes serve a dual function, as scarecrows to deter passing demons during the day, and as rest-stops for tired spirits during the night.

# Incense

Incense has a pleasing smell, and is often used within the Chinese home as an invocation for the protection of ancestors and household gods. However, if you use it within your own home, you must take care not to bring more bad fortune than good. Ash from incense should not be left to fester and bring the bad qi associated with dirt. Also, incense should not be used to excess to remove bad smells. You should remove the bad odor at its source, and not try to obscure it by burning more and more incense. The same applies for any other kind of perfume, be it for your own use or as part of cleaning products.

# Jade

Jade's strange lustrous properties made it an early symbol of magical power. Jade was used to make ceremonial items for prehistoric Chinese religions, and has survived to this day as a symbol of luck and protection. Jade, like any other stone, will break rather than bend, and so it has become a symbol of resolution and unswerving dedication. When jade shatters, it deflects an evil curse. If you want a jade charm, you must receive it as a gift from somebody else; if you buy your own jade items they will have no power. Although jade brings concentration, remember there are some parts of your fortune where a little flexibility is more useful.

# Kites

A kite is considered, for obvious reasons, to be a symbol of aspiration and energy. Kites are thought to encourage the young male children of the house to get out into the fresh air, but because they require skill and a mastery of the winds, they are also a symbol of understanding. A kite in the N sector will encourage successful diplomacy at work. In the NE it is a positive influence on comprehension of studies. In the SE it is a boon to aiding the mastery of finances and investments. Since men in giant kites were once used by the ancient Chinese as scouts, their influence may also ensure that you remain forewarned and forearmed.

# Light

Any form of illumination is a yang influence, scares away evil spirits, and bolsters good qi. Too much will glare and interfere with concentration. Too little can cause misplaced judgement and a waning interest in knowledge and self-improvement. Candles are powerful representations of the Fire element. Incandescent lights (bulbs) are less so, and fluorescent lighting (strips) hardly at all. Lights can be used to create virtual walls; useful for irregularly-shaped houses, where garden lamps can fill in the gap left by a "missing" wall. Artificial light is less beneficial to good qi than natural light, a fact that modern medical science has only recently confirmed, although it has been part of feng shui lore for centuries.

# Maps

Maps are powerful influences on your feng shui, especially in the career (N) or travel (NW) sectors. In ancient times, the Emperor used to keep his map of China on permanent view, on a table in the center of the room so that he and the map could occupy each other's attention constantly. A map not only encourages travel to the place represented, it also encourages a much deeper understanding. It is, after all, pure information hanging in front of the occupant's face, and some of it will doubtless rub off after days of continuous viewing. Old maps are bad luck, since they encourage the occupant to misunderstand the lie of the land.

# Mirrors

One of the most powerful components in feng shui. Increases light and space, and concentrates other components by doubling their appearance. A mirror turned on your books will double your knowledge and concentration. Turned on your money box it will double your savings. But if turned on your trash can it will double your waste. Mirrors should also be used carefully at the office (see Feng Shui in the Workplace), since concentrating workers' attentions on the exit or the coffee machine will reduce their productivity. Use mirrors to "remove" sharp corners, obstructive pillars and cramped alcoves. Since demons are spooked by the sight of their own reflections, a mirror can thwart would-be burglars just inside the doors and windows.

# Ba-Gua

You may have seen strange eight-sided objects used as components in feng shui. These are Ba-Gua symbols ("Ba-Gua" simply means eight sides), which are representations of the eight points of the compass, normally with a mirror in the center and the eight symbols of the Book of Changes fanned around the edge. These Ba-Gua mirrors have to be bought from specialist shops, but are the most powerful feng shui charms of all. If you believe your feng shui to be severely affected by the entry of bad qi through your front door, a Ba-Gua mirror facing it will bounce all evil influences back outside. If a Ba-Gua costs more than a reasonable meal, it is too expensive.

# Pictures

The subject of any picture or sculpture is of paramount importance. Whatever is depicted in the picture will have a very real influence on the occupants of the room. Pictures of animals, for example, will have the same power as the animal itself (see Animals and Pets). Pictures of your ancestors, friends and relatives will involve their spirits in your life, even if they are not physically present. Pictures of famous personalities may be placed in appropriate sectors in order to bestow the same fates and fortunes as those depicted, but take care. If placing a picture of a film star, for example, you must consider not only their own fate, but that of the role they are playing.

## Revolving Objects

The qi of your house needs to be stirred occasionally, like water, in order to keep it fresh and invigorating. Although this is best accomplished though regular airings, it is also aided greatly by revolving objects, which knead the room's qi like slow-moving whisks. Hi-fi systems, clocks, fans, and music boxes all work wonderfully for this. Modern office designers often use revolving doors for a dual purpose, since they allow ease of access to the building and function as weak air-conditioning systems to keep the air constantly circulating. The direction of revolution (clockwise or anti-clockwise) does not affect the circulation of qi; what is important is that it is churned around, not the direction in which this occurs.

# Seasonal Pictures

❀

Some artistic subjects can bring a hidden influence. Pictures or items associated with a particular season will bring that season into your home, and can be used to negate or increase the power of a certain sector. Spring (E), Summer (S), Fall (W) and Winter (N) can be halved or doubled through the addition of the right picture or object. For example, blossoms in the E sector will double the Spring, and hence double the luck in the Family (E) sector. Equally, photographs of the Summer holiday in the N (Winter) sector will bring warmth and joy, and keep back the cold. Spring and Summer are best used for yang (positive) influence, Fall and Winter for yin (negative).

# Shells

❀

The most well-known superstition about these objects in the West is that if you hold certain types of shell to your ear, you are able to hear the sea. In feng shui, too, the presence of a shell can bring a little sea-breeze of calm for those who live far from the water's edge, but they are much better known in China for another association. In ancient China, shells were often used as a form of currency, and so may be used in feng shui as a representation of money. They can encourage riches, especially if placed in the Wealth (SE) sector, and success in business in the N.

# Tables

The dining table plays an important part in family life and is best kept balanced through the number of chairs around it. One-sided dining areas, such as kitchen worktops, discourage social activity, and often have inappropriate seating arrangements (such as high stools) which cramp the occupants into hunching over their food. Remember that the material of the table will be a strong elemental component (e.g. Wood, Metal), and that the shape of the table will also influence the elemental feng shui of a room. A regular shape such as a circle, oblong or rectangle is infinitely preferable to an irregular one. Items left on other tables (such as coffee tables) are on raised plinths, and hence objects of respect.

# Toilet

One of the most difficult concepts for old-style feng shui to embrace has been modern plumbing. In ancient feng shui lore, human waste was part of the natural cycle of existence, used as a fertiliser on crops and hence contributing to the good qi of the universe. In the modern world, it is sequestered in sewers, and, more importantly, flushed down a drain from within the home. As a symbolic exit, the toilet can flush away riches and good luck, and so should always be kept shut when not in use. It is also best kept away from the entrance to the bathroom to shield passers-by; in feng shui, out of sight is literally out of mind.

# Toys

Toys perform a multiplicity of functions associated with childhood. A room or house without children that nevertheless has toys invites the visitor to regard the inhabitants as childish and immature. We all know the joke about leaving roller-skates on the stairs; in feng shui design this isn't funny, because items underfoot will annoy and interfere with the proper activities of the occupants. There are some occasions when the presence of toys may be an advantage, such as when the occupant of a room needs to feel indulged and protected. If placed in the W sector of a house or room, toys may aid in bringing the pitter-patter of tiny feet.

# Trash

All systems create waste that must be disposed of, although perfect systems are able to recycle that which they do not need. Feng shui recycles everything: as good qi loses its energy it slowly stagnates, until it is whipped up again into more good qi in a constant cycle of light and dark, yin and yang. All forms of waste must be disposed of carefully, and the trash can or wastepaper baskets must be placed in strong sectors of the room. Trash in the W sector will create worthless children; in the N a meaningless career; in the NW hangers-on and sycophants. Waste is best kept outside areas of habitation, or at least in a receptacle with a firmly-closed lid.

# Water

It is easy to forget that the Water element does not merely occur naturally in ponds and rivers. Water permeates your household, running through the pipes in the walls, the radiators, and the many faucets in the kitchen and bathroom. It is also found in small quantities in vases of flowers, fish tanks, toilets, and bottles of drink. All of these items may combine to form a greater influence, equivalent to a small stream running through the middle of your house, so do bear them in mind when examining the elemental composition of your house. Steam and water vapor are also strong in the element. Remember that still, stagnant water brings bad qi, and that swirling, active water brings good.

## Willow Pattern

Most Westerners are likely to know of the famous "willow-pattern" crockery, with its distinctive blue and white design. Its associations with China, however, are doubtful to say the least. The full set supposedly portrays a girl's love for her father's secretary, their discovery, elopement, pursuit and the transformation of the lovers into two turtle-doves. The name supposedly comes from the setting of the story at the time when the willow sheds its leaves, but the entire story is likely to be a western concoction made at the design stage. The Chinese do not regard the turtle-dove as a symbol of love and faith, so it is likely that the whole "legend" was dreamed up by a foreign exporter. Powerless in feng shui.

# ANIMALS AND PETS

Human beings are not the only living creatures in a house. Animals are powerful totemistic symbols in feng shui, and come in many forms. Obviously we have the actual creatures themselves as pets, but each of us was also born under a Chinese animal sign. We must also consider the influences of pictures and representations of animals, and of shapes and shadows that resemble animals, for these too will exercise a weak power over the feng shui of your house.

# Bat

飛

Chinese folklore, bereft of a million vampire films to scare it, has a positive attitude towards the humble bat. When in repose, the bat hangs upside down, a habit that seems not to bother it. For this reason, the Chinese regard the bat as a symbol of unique perspective and original inspiration. Bat images in a home will encourage the occupant to look at the world in a different way. Hang them in the N sector to encourage an original approach to a career move, and in the NW to encourage a real change of scene or acquaintances. Since bats are nocturnal creatures, their images encourage occupants to burn the night oil: studying in the NW, laboring in the SE.

# Butterfly

The philosopher Zhuang Zi wondered if he was a man dreaming he was a butterfly, or a butterfly dreaming he was a man. Ever associated with flightiness and feather-weights, the butterfly is a Chinese symbol of a carefree life. It is the butterfly that flits around the garden and enjoys the flowers for what they are, a fact that the hard-working gardener would do well to remember from time to time. Its placement in the home will encourage the occupant to enjoy life and stop taking everything so seriously. In houses which have recently suffered a bereavement, the butterfly is a symbol of the newly-departed soul, and of the occupants' desire that they should rest in peace.

# Cat

The cat is associated with business acumen in China, and many premises have a "lucky cat" placed somewhere near the cash register, with one paw raised up in supplication. In other sectors of your life and luck, the cat is less auspicious. It is a symbol of canny business sense, but also of the will to control and manipulate others, to take without ever giving anything in return. The cat may be a wise creature, but its wisdom is eternally directed at looking after number one, and those who love it can never hope to have their feelings reciprocated. Best avoided, especially in the sectors associated with family and romance.

# Centipede

Moths, butterflies, centipedes and cater-
pillars are not regarded as pests in
China, understandably when you
remember the riches brought by the
humble silk worm. The centipede in
particular is regarded as a very lucky
charm; it is called a "cash-dragon"
because its undulating length resembles a
string of coins. If you find a centipede in
the SE sector of your home or garden, it
is a sure-fire sign of riches around the
corner. If you don't find one, feng shui
lore says you can encourage the fates to
make it happen by putting one there. Do
not kill a centipede within the confines
of your home, it will destroy any riches
you have in the sector where it occurs.

# Cicada/Cricket

In ancient China, the grieving families of
the deceased would place a jade cicada on
their relative's tongue before burial. The
reasoning was that the dead would rise to
new life, just as the cicada, which spends a
large portion of its life underground, rises
from the earth after a long incubation
period. Like the butterfly (see above), the
cicada has become a symbol of regenera-
tion and reincarnation, and can be used
both to ease the passage of a relative into
the next world, and to soothe the grief of
those they leave behind.

# Cormorant

The cormorant was once used in parts of China for fishing. The bird was set off to catch fish in the lake, but had a ring around its thin neck to prevent it swallowing its catch. Cormorants may make for attractive statuary or pictures, but the nature of their employment makes them a little inauspicious. A cormorant image in the N means the occupant will never get the rewards at work that they deserve. In the SE, it may encourage others to skim off the occupant's wealth, in the SW it may encourage the occupant's spouse to stray. In the W sector, it may encourage the occupant's children to be ungrateful and unappreciative. In the S, the occupant may become the subject of gossip.

# Crane

The crane is the bird that carries the soul of the dead to heaven, but in feudal China it became a symbol of justice, because judges had the image of the crane in their courtrooms. Hence, the crane has become a symbol, not of death, but of a just and fitting lifespan, or in other words, a long and happy life. Because the crane's long legs keep it away from the mud, it is also a symbol of purity. In the N sector, it brings reasonable career prospects, in the SE, fitting wealth, in the S fame in keeping with talents. Too many crane symbols may cause the occupants to elevate themselves too high, and become snobbish or overly critical.

# Deer

The deer is said to have found the secret of eternal youth (a kind of mushroom, if the old tales are to be believed). For this reason, many of the Chinese immortals are often to be found riding on, or in the company of deer. But immortality can bring problems of its own; do not use images of the deer unless you are truly happy with the way things are. It will not merely bring long life, but also extend other areas of your fortune. If you are unhappy at work, it will make sure you stay there. If you are in an unhappy relationship, the deer will only prolong the suffering.

# Dog

The dog is one of the signs of the Chinese zodiac, and will exert a powerful influence over occupants born in the Year of the Dog. Dogs are great guardians and watchmen, liable to scare off burglars and other intruders, although sometimes they may misguidedly scare off friends. They can be extremely useful in the W sector as protectors of children, or in the SE as charms against con-artists. If their influence is too powerful within your home, you may find yourself becoming snappy and overprotective. The dog is also a symbol of the element Earth, so take care that its presence or image does not upset the balance of the other elements within your dwelling.

# Dragon

The dragon is another zodiac sign, and one or more of the occupants of your house may have been born in the Year of the Dragon. The dragon is a symbol of the Earth element, and is the most popular symbol in Chinese folklore. The dragon protects, brings luck and success (by flying without wings), and is the divine bringer of storms that clear the air. Chinese dragons are not the evil creatures of Western mythology; as long as they are treated with respect, they will always be kind and friendly to the occupants of a house. The dragon is at its most powerful in the center of a room, but will bring fortune anywhere.

# Duck

※

Ducks, especially the Mandarin duck, are
symbols of marital fidelity because they
mate for life. A powerful image when used
in pairs, the obvious placement is in the
SW (marriage) sector, although the duck
can also be employed in other areas of
feng shui. In the N sector it can bring a
powerful influence to business mergers, in
the W it can bestow good prospects on the
marriages of the occupants' children. If
placed centrally in the room, images or
representations of ducks may cause the
occupants to neglect all else in the pursuit
of love. This may be detrimental to
education and career, but is ultimately
harmless, since a willingness to love love
itself is a sign of enlightenment.

# Elephant

The elephant is a symbol of great wisdom, because it lives to a great old age, and because the Chinese word for elephant ("xiang") rhymes with the word for a minister. Chinese chess is called "Elephant Chess" as a game for wise players. The elephant is also associated with great strength, because it is the largest and most powerful animal on land. Even before the Chinese had heard of the legendary Elephants' Graveyard, they were using statues of these beasts to protect shrines and cemeteries. Useful as a symbol of power and glory, the elephant can be placed in your weakest sector to strengthen and protect it from marauders.

# Fox

Renowned all over the world for its cunning, the fox is greatly feared in the Far East, both for natural and supernatural reasons. Farmers are, of course, concerned about the havoc these creatures can wreak upon unguarded animals, but the fox is notorious in China for wreaking havoc among humans too. Said to be able to change shape, and work mischief, it is a symbol of espionage and intrigue, and in old China it was bad luck to ever say or even write the word "fox." In the N sector it may give you business cunning, but take extreme care with this image, especially if any occupants of the house were born in the Year of the Rooster.

# Frog

The frog (or toad, Chinese folklore does not really distinguish between them) can encourage great leaps of activity, although not necessarily in the right direction. It can also be a symbol of misguided ideas, since thanks to the bulging set of the eyes, the higher a frog stands on its hind legs, the less it sees except what is actually behind it. Frogs are sometimes used in feng shui designs to encourage quick thinking and fast reactions, but you are advised to look before you leap.

# Fish

🜍

Goldfish are thought by some to be infant dragons, who achieve their final form when they pass through the gates of heaven. Kindness to a goldfish is repaid ten-fold after its death (a reward for the protection of a dragon), but a bad pet-owner can expect to suffer mightily if his goldfish returns to haunt him. Dying is not important for goldfish (since they are bound to return), but the living of a good life is, so owners should make sure their fish are well-kept. Carp and salmon are symbols of youthful effort, because they strive to swim upstream, and are powerful charms in the NE (study) or N (career) sectors. Dolphins and whales count as fish, even though they are mammals.

# Giraffe

The graceful giraffe has always been associated by the Chinese with beauty, ever since the first Chinese explorers in Africa were entertained by its preening antics. The two stubby horns make it seem like a distant relation of the long-living deer, but it is the legs and extended neck that give it its real power. The giraffe is perfectly suited to its environment, and a symbol of contentment. If there are any sectors in your feng shui that you feel are truly, absolutely perfect, then a giraffe might keep them that way. The giraffe has trouble getting to its feet after a fall, so a broken giraffe image can ruin your fortune in the sector where the accident occurs.

# Hare/Rabbit

The hare is one of the twelve signs of the Chinese zodiac, and a symbol of the element Wood. Hare imagery in the home brings a prosperous life and quick thinking, but may also encourage slap-dash ideas. Like its leaping counterpart the frog, the hare is apt to act without thinking and may rest on its laurels. The Chinese know the story of the Tortoise and the Hare, and warn that too many images of this swift creature will bring quantity ahead of quality. A single red hare, however, is a sign of good fortune. It will bring particular benefits if placed in the W sector (children) or SW (marriage), although occupants hoping for a *small* family should avoid it.

# Horse

The horse is one of the twelve signs of the Chinese zodiac, and a symbol of the element Fire. An animal greatly revered in Asia for the power brought to Genghis Khan by his cavalry, the horse is a symbol of hardy endurance, a willingness to work, but also of occasional fits of temper (as you might expect from a creature ruled by Fire). A horse will benefit study in the NE sector, and career in the N. In the SW, it will aid marriage because it is also a symbol of loyalty. An image of race-horses emphasises speed over endurance. Never place a horse and a deer side by side; a "horse-deer" is a Japanese "idiot."

# Monkey

﷼

The monkey is one of the twelve signs of the Chinese zodiac, and ruled by the element Metal. In Chinese legend, it was the Monkey King who stole the peaches of immortality from the Divine Emperor's garden, and the monkey has always been associated with tricks and jokes. His inherent playfulness is sometimes welcome; in fact, it may be all that is required in the E or W sector to drag children out of a depression or illness and back to normality. However, the monkey is notorious for playing all day and never working, and a monkey influence (including baboons, gorillas and chimpanzees) in the study or career sectors could spell disaster for the occupant who wants to get ahead.

# Ox

The ox is another of the twelve signs of the Chinese zodiac, ruled by the element Earth. The loyal creature that pulls the plow and cart, the ox is associated with help and friendship. It is a strong talisman for bringing friends in time of need, especially if placed in the NW sector. The drawback with oxen and representations of oxen is that they can be a little stubborn, and may need to be encouraged with a few stern tugs. This is particularly likely during the winter months, when traditionally cattle had little else to do but sit around munching on food and fattening themselves for an unknown fate. Too many oxen motifs can make you complacent and gullible.

# Peacocks

꫞

A feather from a peacock's tail would be bestowed by the Manchu emperors as a badge of achievement. Each "eye" on the peacock's tail-feather would represent another honor for which the recipient had been thanked. For this reason, peacock's feathers are signs of great accomplishments, and bring great fame in the S sector, and much success in the workplace if placed in the N. However, the peacock is also a sign of a vain male, interested in nothing except impressing the local womenfolk, so such representations are best kept out of the NE sector (a dangerous distraction during examinations) and the SW in the approach to a marriage (for the groom should put his flirting days behind him).

# Phoenix

If the dragon is the powerful, male symbol of China, then the phoenix is the nurturing, female symbol. It is also a strong Water influence because of its purity. The phoenix only appears in times of great prosperity, but is said to grant long happiness, happy marriages, and a thriving peace throughout the world. Its images are particularly strong in the SW (marriage) sector, but will bring harmony to all the others. A symbol of eternal life because it is constantly reborn, the phoenix happily sacrifices itself because it knows it will return. Too much phoenix imagery around your home may encourage some occupants (especially the lady of the house) to compromise too much and believe that nobody appreciates them.

# Pig

Another Chinese zodiac sign, the pig is greatly revered in China, both for its meat and its legendary sensitivity. A symbol of family happiness (the Chinese character for "family" is a pig under a roof), it is also ruled by the Water element. The pig in feng shui is a softening component, used to soothe and calm enemies and potential problems. It will ease a troubled atmosphere at work in the N, bring compassionate friends in the NW and pour oil on troubled marital waters in the SW, but take care that it is not used to excess. Overuse of pig or Water images will make the occupants of a room oversensitive, easily hurt and quick to take offense.

# Rat

The smallest animal represented in the Chinese zodiac, the rat is ruled by the element Water. The rat in Chinese folklore is a smooth and cunning operator, a charmer, and a cad. A wise counsellor to all except himself, he is a keen gambler, especially with other people's money. The rat can also be a sign of greed, and is best kept out of all sectors of your feng shui. The only exception is where a member of your household was born in the Year of the Rat, in which case its image may aid their fortune when placed in the appropriate sector. Rat imagery is best kept away from representations of the Snake, since they are natural enemies.

# Rooster

A proud and feisty sign of the Chinese zodiac, the rooster is ruled by the element Metal. Fiercely protective of his family, the rooster is the chivalrous knight among the animals; with a crown on his head and spurs on his feet, he combines images of nobility and courage. Still used as a fighting creature in Asia, the rooster brings pride and daring into whichever sector it finds itself. Nervous job applicants should place rooster imagery in the N sector to steel their resolve, timid suitors should place it in the SW to help them pop the question. But if the rooster imagery is used to excess, it will make the occupants boastful and cocksure, and pride still goes before a fall.

# Sheep/Goat

羊

The sheep is another sign of the Chinese zodiac, and one ruled by the element Earth. Kind-hearted and gentle, sheep are naturally successful in business because they produce wool without any effort. For this reason, sheep imagery is particularly powerful in the N and SE to encourage business success, but should not be used too often. Sheep are notoriously indecisive, and can run into trouble without a strong shepherd. If you have to make an important choice in life, keep sheep imagery away from your feng shui. In Chinese astrology, the sheep is sometimes replaced by a goat, and this works in feng shui too. Sheep are best kept away from those born in the Year of the Tiger.

# Snake

Sometimes called the "little dragon" of the Chinese zodiac, the snake is ruled by the element Fire. The snake is a fiercely intelligent creature, highly manipulative and a true believer in the pre-emptive strike for dealing with enemies before they even become enemies. A bad influence on friendship, but not necessarily so in business, the snake's charm and cleverness can work wonders in the appropriate sectors. Best kept out of the W (children) and SW (marriage), because the snake will always be a predator and a sneak. May bring success in business in the N, but it may also bring hazards, for who will be the cunning schemer to benefit? Will it be you, or your enemies?

# Tiger

The tiger is another sign of the Chinese zodiac, and ruled by the Wood element because its favorite hunting ground is amid the trees of the forest. Chinese warriors painted the image of the tiger on their shields, hoping to use the feng shui representation to bring some of the tiger's warlike spirit into their own souls. The tiger is a symbol of bold leadership, and a powerful influence if you are already in charge of something. If you are not, it is a symbol of dissension, because, like all cats, the tiger does not follow orders willingly. Keep tiger imagery away from new arrivals, especially if they were born in the Year of the Hare, Pig or Rooster.

# Tortoise/Turtle

One of the sacred animals of China, the tortoise is a symbol of great longevity, and of slow but sure effort and improvement. A story was told in ancient times that the tortoise had forgotten the Eight Rights and Wrongs: its image in the W will make children behave, but in the SW it will make the lady of the house misbehave. The tortoise's shell makes it a symbol of impregnability, but also of unsuspected flaws, for how is the tortoise to know what will happen when it is upended? A hill behind your house in the N is said to protect it like a turtle's shell. A turtle image in the NW may help combat impotence.

# Unicorn

The Chinese unicorn or jilin (called a "kirin" in Japan, and still a brand of Japanese beer) is a sign of peace and wise rulership. It also bestows fame and fortune upon the children of a household, and is most powerful when placed in the W (children) sector. Even when their children have grown up and left home, many Chinese couples still place a unicorn image in the W to bring luck to their offspring, and, by association, to themselves. If the occupants of a house are plagued by an important decision, the unicorn image will help them make the correct choice. The Western image of the unicorn is a reasonable substitute if you cannot find the Chinese variety.

# Wolf

The wolf is seen as a kind of dog, yet wilder, and as a kind of tiger, but more co-operative. It is also regarded, mainly in the old rural communities, as a pest and a predator like the fox. In feng shui it remains a symbol of the loner and the hermit, and possibly of a noble warrior unjustly cast out of loyal service. The wolf is a powerful image to use in your feng shui at times when it appears all others are against you. It may be lonely in the dark forest, but the dawn will come, and with it, absolution. If used to excess, wolf imagery may cause a violent temper.

# NUMBERS

Numbers play an important part in feng shui, and the number of similar objects in a room may influence the kind of fortune they bring. Just as two's company and three's a crowd in our own folklore, the numbers game in the Chinese world comes fraught with superstitions and old wives' tales.

There is not enough space in this book to deal with every single number in the world, but this chapter examines the most common superstitions and charms, both for counting the objects in your home, and also for external influences like your home address. When it comes to large numbers, like your phone or bank account, it is the last few digits that contain the fortune, since you can't change your area code without moving house.

# One

There is only one World, and so one is a symbol of exclusivity and uniqueness. It represents the height of achievement, but in the gregarious and sociable Chinese worldview, it is not a number that can be encouraged or maintained for long. There is a loneliness to command, and while one represents achievement, it can also represent isolation. One item from a pair signifies that something has gone amiss; make sure that all single items are not supposed to have a friend to keep them company. A single chair does not invite company, but a single chair built for two invites companionship, and perhaps even flirtation. A single bed invites sleeping alone, whether you want to or not.

# Two

Every couple is made of two, an obvious observation but nevertheless an important reason behind the significance of Chinese gift-giving. At weddings especially, the gift of a pair of *anything* is apt to encourage romance and happiness. Pairs of pictures or statues are best balanced by a single object in between them, and the doubling of objects normally found singly will increase their influence. This is one reason why mirrors are used, to symbolically "double" the amount of light, wealth, or happiness in a room. There is a downside, that pairs of unsightly or inauspicious objects will bring double the bad luck. A house in between two cemeteries, for example, is unlikely to thrive and prosper.

# Three

In Chinese thought, the number three is associated with stability, because ancient tripods were considered the stablest of objects. From stability, Chinese folklore has moved on to associate the number three with longevity, and with expansion. A line between two points is just a line, but connecting three it gains an extra dimension. For this reason, three can signify an extra point of view for added value. A patient only has a doctor's word to believe in; the addition of a second opinion is in actuality the addition of a third party. The Chinese numeral three, which looks like III turned on its side, also resembles the strongest "yang" (positive) symbol from the Book of Changes.

# Four

Four *should* be a lucky number because it is composed of two pairs, and hence a doubling of a doubling. But the Chinese word for four "si" is the same as the Chinese word for death, and the number is avoided at all costs. Some Chinese buildings do not have fourth floors, but leap straight from three to five since nobody would ever install an office or apartment in such an inauspicious place. Some Chinese streets do not even have a house number four. The number four is as carefully avoided in the East as the number thirteen is in the West, although it does occasionally appear in the complex numerological school of feng shui, for experts only.

# Five

𹉢

Imperial dragons have five claws, because they require a thumb to write letters and turn the pages of books. There are five major points to the Chinese compass, because the four directions require a center to unite them. China also has five mountains considered sacred, all of which combine to make five a very lucky number indeed. Associated in feng shui with the power of the emperor, the magic of the dragon, and the strength and calm of the center, five and multiples of five are auspicious on phone numbers, houses, and floors of buildings. For the average family, five chairs around a table encourages guests and helpers to come round for dinner.

# Six

Thanks to a pun in Chinese which rhymes six ("liu") with the word for affluence, this is also a lucky number, even more so because it is twice three. It also rhymes with the word for remaining far away, and can be used in the NE sector to encourage foreign study, and in the NW to encourage travel. There are six domestic animals in Chinese folklore (the horse, ox, sheep, hen, dog and pig), and the use of sixes in the E or SW sectors encourages calm and domesticity in the home. Chinese folklore does not share the Western, Christian obsession with 666 being the number of the Beast; it is in fact regarded as a very lucky number indeed.

# Seven

There are seven stars in the Big Dipper, a constellation which has given birth to an entire spin-off school called Seven Star Feng Shui. Seven times seven (49), is the number of days prescribed for an acceptable period of mourning, but this has not led to its association with death and sadness. Instead, it has become the number of reasonable effort, said to show loyalty and understanding, and a general respect for the spirits, making seven a very magical number. This magical association is something which also exists in our own culture, where for centuries the powers of sorcery and divination have been ascribed to those who are the "seventh sons of seventh sons."

# Eight

Two separate religious traditions in China value eight, since there are eight Buddhist treasures and eight Taoist immortals. The octagon as a shape is the most powerful magical protector in the feng shui home (see Furniture and Objects), and an eight-sided table is a particularly strong artefact. Quantities of eight are excellent things to wipe out weak sectors in your feng shui, be they actual collections of eight objects, pictures of them, or items with eight sides such as a vase or plate. Eight is also considered lucky because it is two times two times two, or two to the power of three, both combinations of even more lucky numbers. You really cannot go wrong with this number.

# Nine

There are eight points on the compass, plus the center to make nine, the feng shui number associated with totality and wholeness. Whereas five is a number for strength and power, nine is three times three times three, and its Chinese word ("jiu") rhymes with the words for longevity and alcoholic drink. For this reason, nine is associated with a full and happy life, living to a ripe old age, and a career path and history that shows the occupant fulfilling each and every one of his or her wishes. With a life full of nines, the occupant cannot fail in meeting each of their desires, because nine means completeness above all else.

# Other Numbers

❀

The use of the decimal system has led the Chinese to associate ten with completeness and luck. Similarly, the number thirteen has bad connotations in feng shui, not because of China, but because of the West's influence on it. Other numbers can be made from the lower numbers, and are particularly lucky if they can be reformed to make multiples of nine. So 369 contains three lucky numbers, and can be added to make 18, a multiple of nine, and the one and eight can be added in turn to make another nine. Other numbers are puns: 928 means "easy growth," 28 means "prosperity" and 48 means "expansion." But beware 174, "yi qi si" or "dying together."

# THE VIEW FROM YOUR WINDOW

The window is not merely a yang influence, letting in light. It is also part of the wall and part of the room's decoration. Anything that can be seen through the window will enter the room's feng shui as if it is inside the room itself, and so the view from your house should be carefully policed.

Sometimes it is best to curtain off inauspicious windows, or even to block them up entirely. Conversely, if there is a fabulously auspicious view on one side of your house, why not enlarge the window to bring you more luck on that side? The view will be most influential on its sector, e.g. N window (career), SW (marriage) etc. Here are just some of the views you may have outside your house.

# The Natural World

꽃

The best possible view you can hope to have will be one of the natural world. Home-owners are encouraged by feng shui masters to make full use of the viewing opportunities offered by their gardens, through bay windows, conservatories and verandas. If you do not have a large garden, particularly at the front of your house, you can encourage similar qi through window boxes, vines, and screens of trees and shrubs. In urban and suburban areas, a wall of trees will also act as a noise wall, helping to reduce pollution by sound as well as bad qi. If your view is landscaped, ensure it does not fall into disrepair, or your fortune will follow suit.

# Shapes

Naturally-occurring phenomena and other buildings may have distinctive shapes, making them as much a part of your room's elemental feng shui as the material from which your house is built and the colors of the decoration. See under The Five Elements for more details, but as an example, a building with a triangular roof will represent the element Fire. Make sure that this is an acceptable element in that sector of the room, and balance or obscure it if it is not. Although pyramidal structures have a triangular sides and a square base, their influence is negative, since they are houses of the dead.

# Shadows

As the trees in the forest struggle in a competition for sunlight, the buildings in a city struggle to remain out of the shadows. If you live in a city dominated by huge skyscrapers, check that you are not living in the shadow of the taller buildings. It is not merely a case of getting more sunlight, you will also have to deal with bad qi tumbling down from on high, and the possibility that the mirrored surfaces and sharp edges will all be bouncing bad qi in your direction. If you are living inside one of the larger buildings, check that it has a regular shape; the 1970s vogue for strangely shaped buildings is no good for feng shui.

# Types of Building

Pay particular attention to the type of building you can see. Empty buildings are considered bad feng shui, and if you are moving into a building that has been empty for a long time you should let off some fire crackers to scare away the evil spirits who may have gathered. A car park is another kind of emptiness, and one which encourages people to stop off on their way to do more interesting things. A view of the car park will encourage others to use you as a facility, but not as a destination. It is best avoided. Empty lots are part of the natural world, but a lot that exists to be empty is a very bad view indeed.

# Sky

A view of the sky or clouds and nothing else might sound strange, but is easily achieved with highly placed windows or sky-lights. This view encourages the occupants of a room to believe that the sky really is the limit, and they will strive hard in any venture in which they find themselves involved. However, take care that every single view is not of such a kind; while this would encourage the occupants to aspire to lofty heights indeed, it would also cause them to spend a lot of time with their heads in the clouds, and you may find that they become distant and out of touch with reality. What use are your accomplishments if locked in an ivory tower?

# Hills

A view of hills is generally a good thing, especially if they undulate. But if the house stands at the base of a very tall hill that blocks the view entirely, the qi is much less auspicious. The presence of the hill not only blocks the regular flow of qi from auspicious locations behind it, but funnels bad influences right at the house. Just as dry desert valleys are to be avoided at all costs during rainstorms, so must the occupants of such a house prepare themselves for constant downpours of bad luck, and inundations of misfortune. The placement of mirrors might alleviate some of the risk, but this is a location that should really be avoided from the outset.

# Holy Places

A view of a cemetery, no matter how pretty the surroundings, is considered to be a bad thing, since restless spirits may wander up to the house to cause mischief. There is much less risk if your own ancestors are buried in the cemetery, since it will be a mark of respect that each of you can look over the other. Although churches and other places of worship have a positive image in our society, to feng shui masters the good is canceled out by the many spirits that will flock to such a place. Matters are not helped by steeples and crucifixes, which are sharp objects and hence generators of pointed, bad qi.

# Hospitals and Police Stations

𝍠

For similar reasons, the joy of birth and healing at a hospital is off-set by the pain of death and illness. It's too risky to try for one without encouraging the other. You might expect a view of a police station to be a good thing, since it would encourage law-abiding behaviour, and function as an excellent sort of protection. However, feng shui lore reminds us that the police at such a station are outnumbered by criminals, who are a much less positive influence. For the same reason, a prison is a very inauspicious view, especially because the occupants of the house may constantly fret and worry about escaped convicts, and cause themselves extra stress.

# Factories

As areas of bustle and industry, you might think that factories would appeal to the hard-working Chinese. But factories are also places of misery and hardship, and because of the costs of the plant and machinery, are likely to run twenty-four hours a day, polluting your luck with noise and distraction. Factories with tall chimneys resemble sticks of incense burning at a funeral, feng shui lore says if you look at them for too long the funeral could be yours! When all is said and done, you're better off away from the factory location; if you must see industry at work, see something natural and old-fashioned such as farming (close to nature) or education (inspiring and youthful).

# Trash and Dumpsters

Seemingly innocent items from everyday life can also cause bad qi if seen from the windows. Large receptacles for trash are unfavorable, both because they can give off unpleasant odors, and because people disposing of waste will invariably drop some in the surrounding area. Recycling bins bring a similar danger, although their characteristic dome-like shapes help contain the waste and the bad qi it generates. As with trash cans within the home, a lid on the bad qi is half the battle. Despite this, even a view of beneficial objects such as recycling bins is to be discouraged, since the noise as passers-by throw glass bottles into them does not abate during the night, and can prevent restful sleep.

# Bus Stops

Although many Western estate agents like to advertize their properties as "convenient for buses," the Chinese would prefer the bus stop to be out of sight. This is because the traditional shape of a bus stop, like a steel flag atop a long pole, reminds the Chinese of an axe about to fall. This is a particularly deadly influence, since it is not merely the image of sharpness, but that the steel flag is genuinely dangerous (I speak as someone who once collided with a bus stop head-on!) Of course, if the bus stop is that close, you will have the added distraction of the traffic grinding into motion all hours of the day and night.

## Traffic Roundabouts

Like the roundabout used for children's recreation (see Swings and Roundabouts), the traffic roundabout is an essentially good object. It eases the flow of cars and other vehicles without the artificial "Stop" commands of traffic lights, and encourages the traffic to circulate like a benevolent water feature. Although any rural feature is preferable to an urban one like traffic, this particular feature will bring less bad fortune than any other, and if it comes with a small garden in the center, so much the better, since a little of the countryside is better than nothing.

# Trains and Subways

There are several adverse influences from the railroad, the most obvious of which are the continuous noise, distractions, and vibration from the clanking trains as they go past. There are also the hazardous power cables to consider, which are regarded as dangerous by both feng shui masters and Western scientists. If you can see the entrance to a subway from your door, it works like a drain on your good qi and is best obscured by trees or curtains. There is also a physical influence on your life, which is that every time you leave your door you will have to fight your way past all the commuters converging on the entrance.

# Poles and Pylons

Like trees of negativity in the urban world, telegraph poles and electrical pylons are best avoided. They hold power cables precariously above your home and street, and are connected to each other in crowded urban areas in a network that resembles a spider's web, in which your house and fortune can be caught. Telegraph poles in some countries have a hoop of white paint around their midriff; for the Chinese it resembles a white arm-band worn for mourning. Such items should be removed from your sight as quickly as possible, and can be "buried" beneath a view of other trees, or simply covered up altogether with curtains or the removal of the offending window.

# Swings and Roundabouts

❀

A view of a children's playground is a good thing. The Chinese love children, and regard the sounds of their happy play to be a rejuvenating and calming influence. It helps too that it is an area of well-kept, landscaped ground designed for pleasure and relaxation. As long as the playground is in good repair, it should bring you fortune, especially since the roundabouts will whisk up the local qi when they are spun. But beware swings facing your house (their guillotine movement sends cutting qi towards you) and slides facing you head-on (since they will channel bad qi). The more grass and growing things, the better; a concrete playground is not good for qi.

# Bridges

A view of a bridge from your window is not necessarily a bad thing. Bridges join opposing halves to make a whole, and are consequently symbols of communication and unity. Matters are different, however, if the bridge actually arches over your house, because this is very bad feng shui indeed. A house beneath a bridge will be symbolically stepped on by people passing overhead, and also risks falling debris as passers-by throw rubbish over the side. By being beneath the bridge, and hence neither origin or destination, it is a symbol of being left out of the loop. People go from A to B, but your house is at C, where they never come calling.

# Clothes-Lines

If a room looks out upon your back yard, there is a chance it may see your clothes-line. Some people, in these tumble-dry days, have no need of a clothes-line at all, while others may have the rotating variety, which is very good feng shui because it is a revolving object, and a useful component for stirring qi. But the more traditional style of clothes-line should not be visible from your window. It resembles a trap or garrotte strung across your fortune, and you should take care that it does not strangle you as you go about your daily business. Such lines are particularly dangerous across the path or facing a door, because they are a more direct influence.

# Water-Courses

Even in urban areas, there are several types of stream and river that may influence the feng shui of your house. Large storm drains will also function as drains for your luck, and should be avoided if their entrances face your door. A key problem with urban areas is that naturally-occurring rivers, which are very good for rural feng shui, are diverted, trapped, or otherwise sunk out of sight, and invariably used as part of the city's drainage network. So, from being a happy, sparkling brook of good qi, many urban rivers are turned into sunken, sullen, open drains, with no freedom to move and no chance of vigor. This will have the equivalent effect on your luck and fortune.

# Roofs

If you can see the roof of another house from your window, make sure that you have taken the necessary precautions. If the slope of the roof is not facing you, then there will not be any problems. But if the slope of the roof is facing you, it might have sharp pointed eaves or even a high enough angle that it will resemble a knife cutting into your house. Houses with curved, Oriental-style eaves will slow down the passage of negative qi, but may also function like ramps, dumping bad qi from above into your own garden. If there is a risk of this, ensure there are plenty of exits lest evil spirits get out through your house.

# Fencing

Fences with pointed, vertical slats or stakes create sharp, bad qi, and are also symbolic of the element Fire (for the triangular tips). In feng shui terms, such a fence will generate a wall of flame around your home; it may be protective, but it will also heat tempers within. The alternative fencing with rounded tips is a symbol of the element Metal, but unfortunately also resembles the shape of a Chinese tombstone (which is a tall, thin stone pillar). This will attract many spirits to your area, but good spirits are busy caring for their descendants, so you will be stuck with the bad spirits with time on their hands and mischief in mind.

# Chains

There are other kinds of fence, chiefly the chain-link variety that functions like a net around your house. In some lines of business, this can bring great bounty as it trawls for suitable catches. It is also friendly towards vines and creepers, creating a natural wall reinforced with the element Metal. Small symbolic walls consisting of chains strung between stumps are much less auspicious. Because they really are made of chains, they will tie up and weigh down your fortune as if it is a captured criminal. You may find yourself rooted to the spot and unable to move. No matter how many times you sign contracts or accept promotions, events will conspire to keep you right where you are.

# Walls

**※**

The Great Wall of China had a dual purpose. For many years, it kept the barbarian nomads out (until the day that it didn't). But it also reminded the Chinese on the other side that once they crossed the line, they were no longer under the protection of the Emperor. Walls can keep people out, but they also keep people in. If your house's feng shui is suitably auspicious, walls, especially small ones, help keep in the luck. But if your fortune is bad, you will be grateful there are exits, otherwise you will be trapped in your asylum as surely as if you were in a lift trapped between two floors. Remember bricks are made of the Earth element.

# Junctions

✺

The T-junction is one of the most inauspicious arrangements in urban feng shui. Bad luck and evil spirits, traveling in straight lines, can smack right into your front door, not to mention speeding cars that haven't noticed the signs. The chances of a crash waking you up at night are greatly increased, and the headlights of oncoming cars may be able to shine right in through your window. Walls and lines of trees are one of the best remedies if you find yourself in this unfortunate situation. Another good idea is to shift your front door so that it does not face the oncoming traffic (be it actual or spiritual). It could save your life, or luck.

# The Sea

❀

The Chinese recognize that the sea is a powerful force of good qi and natural energy, but prefer not to be too close to it lest they be overwhelmed. As a distant view from your window, the sea is a beautiful and powerful charm for luck and well-being, but the ancient Chinese fear of floods and storms precludes being too close to it. China is such a large country that for entire periods of its history it never looked outwards to foreign lands. The presence of the sea is a reminder of invaders and pirates to some feng shui masters, and they advise that you, like generations of Chinese people, should be far enough from it to be safe.

# Advertising

❀

Modern city-dwellers may say that they are not affected by advertising on television and billboards, but they could not be more wrong. After all, what is feng shui if not an ancient form of spiritual advertising, designed to "sell" you on the idea of living a good and happy life? If you don't believe in the power to persuade, you cannot believe in feng shui. But if you do, you will know that the presence of a billboard outside your house may influence you over time to do what you are told. It will also function as a wall, blocking the passage of qi. This can be good if it obscures an even more unfavorable view, otherwise avoid.

# FENG SHUI IN THE WORKPLACE

❀

Feng shui does not merely influence your home life, it influences every aspect of your day-to-day existence. For this reason, feng shui principles will also apply strongly in your place of work, especially since for some people this will be a symbolic second home.

The points of the compass will be just as powerful an influence at work, as will the standard feng shui rules on color, objects and views. Noises and distractions are just as unwelcome at work as they are at home, as are unfavorable situations such as placement on a T-junction. There are also one or two special rules specifically for business feng shui included in the next few pages.

# Location

🦋

Location is everything: eye-catching exteriors will draw people into your shop out of curiosity. The best place to be is somewhere where the customers find themselves walking towards it, as opposed to past it. People, like qi, are more favorable to businesses when they can move in slow swirls. A large, well-appointed shopping district allows people to meander from place to place, which is preferable to a business located by a busy road, where potential customers will speed past in a straight, bad-qi line without even noticing you are there. Ensure that you can capture qi and customers alike by siting your business somewhere it can be seen and noticed.

# Mirrors

We have already discussed the use of
mirrors in the home as demon-warding
objects, and reflectors for bad qi. In the
Chinese business world, mirrors are used
to double quantities of favorable items.
Many Chinese restaurants and shops have
a mirror placed close to the cash register
to symbolically double their cashflow, and
large, full-length wall mirrors are also
used to symbolically double the number
of customers in the shop. In offices,
mirrors should not draw workers' attention to the exit or any other influence that
would distract them from their duties.
Workers will lose productivity if their eyes
are drawn to the coffee machine, canteen,
smoking area or toilets every time they
look up.

# Seating

In large company environments such as a typing pool or open-plan office, the manager should be in a commanding position that oversees the entire staff. Staff with better hopes of promotion should be able to gain his or her attention without undue effort, and are best placed close to the manager. The closer a worker is to the manager and the further from the door, the greater the chances of promotion and success. If a worker is on the far side of the room, close to the exit, they risk misfortune and dismissal. Secretaries and assistants should always be closer to the door than the boss. The longer your walk from the door to the desk, the more important you must be.

# Desks

Your desk can be arranged along feng shui principles just as if it were a room itself. Place objects in the appropriate sectors (the phone in the NW for helpful people, for example), but do be sensible. You should not have to cross your arms to answer the phone or get material, so a lot of your desk organization may change depending on whether you are right- or left-handed. Do not sit at your desk with your back to the door. In ancient China this was a maxim to protect you from sneak attacks, in the business world it pays to know what is approaching, and an eye on your colleagues will help keep you alert.

# Tables

✸

The proprietors of restaurants and other eateries are reminded that the number four is very unlucky in feng shui. Many Chinese restaurants avoid seating four at a table by using two small tables, set closely together, but without quite touching. If you are ever seated in such a fashion, the owner of the restaurant is not trying to separate you from your companions, but is symbolically seating you in two pairs of lucky two, rather than a single grouping of the unlucky four. Circular tables encourage community and chat, but should not be too large lest the diners are forced to shout across at each other. Eating alone is discouraged in feng shui, because food should bring people together.

# Water

The people of Hong Kong associate "water" with "money" because to them it is a pun (the pun does not work in English). But the sound of flowing water is soothing, as the modern-day purveyors of ambient relaxation tapes have shown. Perhaps a fountain in your hotel's foyer might not literally bring in money, but it might encourage customers to return time and again to enjoy your soothing environment. And if they do, the more money your business will make. Water absorbs bad qi and generates good, and will be an extra special charm if it contains goldfish: eight gold for luck, and one black for protection. If the black fish dies, it will have saved you from a terrible fate.

# AFTERWORD

Feng shui cannot be fully contained in this little book, for it is as wide and diverse as China itself. Everyone has their own ideas about what works for them, and even in the Chinese community, the seriousness with which feng shui is regarded often varies.

That said, it is a rare Chinese business indeed that does not call in a feng shui master before it opens its doors. It is the architectural equivalent of a medical check-up, since even those businessmen who believe themselves to be above superstition would rather be safe than sorry. Even in our modern age, we need our own feng shui masters. How many really understand the mysterious ways of the architect, the surveyor or the interior decorator? Indeed, how many of us really comprehend everything the doctor tells us about our state of health? We like to believe that we are living in a rational age, but we have merely reassigned the magician's job to the scientist.

The feng shui masters were the scientists of their day, and although many of their ideas have been discredited, a much greater number have remained with us. Today, we think of them as common sense, but it was the feng shui masters that first had that sense. Who is to say that tomorrow, or next week, or next year, a supposedly crazy piece of feng shui lore will be found to contain a grain of truth? It has happened thousands of times before, and doubtless will happen many times more.

It has been said that the sign of a truly advanced civilization is that its technology is indistinguishable from magic. When we delve into the mysterious world of feng shui, with its weather magic, divination, rules for siting houses, and advice on color schemes, we find ourselves working with a magic that is indistinguishable from technology. In one sense, the feng shui masters are thousands of years behind us. But they were right much more often than they were wrong, and who is to say that their rules won't be right for you?

There is only one way to find out for sure, and that is to experiment with feng shui for yourself. Change some colors, move some items, think about your house and garden, and see if your changes bring any more good fortune into your life. If they do, was it positive thinking or the power of suggestion? Or was it magic? It is all these things. It is none of them. And that is feng shui.

# APPENDIX:
# THE BA-GUA

Listed below are all the permutations of the ba-gua. Each sector of your home rules a particular aspect of your life, a member of your family, or a part of the body. If they are not balanced, they could cause trouble in those areas. If you plan them right, they can bring you good fortune.

Check that the area is not blocked or cramped, and if it is, symbolically expand it with a mirror. Also make sure that there are no objects or pictures in that sector that have unfortunate connotations (you can do this by checking the colors and artefacts in this book). If your room (and by association, your life) seems well-balanced already, perhaps you would like to improve matters by placing charms to positively influence your life. This book has plenty of suggestions, but once you get going, the sky really is the limit. If something isn't covered here, why not experiment by placing it in a sector to see if it brings any changes in the next few weeks.

Each sector is listed as follows:

Direction's name: (e.g. North, South, etc.)
Ruling aspect: (the area that will be improved with a positive feng shui aspect, and damaged if the area's feng shui is unfavorable)
Body part: (the part of the occupant's body that is likely to be positively/negatively affected by good/bad feng shui in the area)
Color: (the shade that brings the most qi energy to the sector)
Family member: (the family member likely to be positively/negatively affected)

Element: (the Chinese element in which the sector is already strong. Add the element, its representation or its color to increase strength if the sector's power appears to be waning)

North
Career and career prospects
Ears
Black
Young man or adult son
Water

North East
Knowledge/self-improvement
Hand
Black/blue/green
Young boy or youngest son
Earth (weak)

East
Family/health
Foot

Green
Adult son or mature male
Wood (strong)

South East
Wealth
Hips
Blue/purple/red
Eldest daughter
Wood (weak)

South
Fame/rank
Eye
Red
Young lady or adult daughter
Fire

South west
Marriage
Internal organs
Red/pink/white
Older woman or mother

Earth (strong)

West
Children
Mouth
White
Young girl or youngest daughter
Metal (weak)

North west
Mentors, Helpful people, travel, networking
Head
White/grey/black
Older man or father
Metal (strong)

Center
General well-being
Torso
Yellow
The whole family
Earth (very strong)